Writing Home, With Love

Writing Home, With Love

Politics for Neighbors and Naysayers

Amy Laura Hall

 CASCADE *Books* · Eugene, Oregon

WRITING HOME, WITH LOVE
Politics for Neighbors and Naysayers

Cascade Books
An Imprint of Wipf and Stock Publishers
199 W. 8th Ave., Suite 3
Eugene, OR 97401

www.wipfandstock.com

PAPERBACK ISBN: 978-1-4982-8262-8
HARDCOVER ISBN: 978-1-4982-8264-2
EBOOK ISBN: 978-1-4982-8263-5

Cataloguing-in-Publication data:

Names: Hall, Amy Laura.

Title: Writing home, with love : politics for neighbors and naysayers / Amy Laura Hall.

Description: Eugene, OR: Cascade Books, 2016

Identifiers: ISBN 978-1-4982-8262-8 (paperback) | ISBN 978-1-4982-8264-2 (hardcover) | ISBN 978-1-4982-8263-5 (ebook)

Subjects: LCSH: 1. Political theology. | 2. Community development. | I. Title.

Classification: BR115.P7 H3255 2016 (paperback) | CALL NUMBER (ebook)

Manufactured in the U.S.A.   11/15/16

For Emily and Rachel

CONTENTS

STAND IN THE PLACE WHERE YOU LIVE

My dad is a Methodist minister. So, we moved like hoboes when I was young. My great-grandmother told me I grew up "Black Dutch." She told me this with defiant pride, because she was part of that heritage. When I tried to sort this out using a dictionary, the word that came up repeatedly was (and still is) the impolitic term "Gypsy."

I grew up under what is called the "itinerate system." This is the formal way of saying that a Methodist bishop moves a pastor from church to church, depending on the needs of particular churches in a region. This is supposed to teach Methodists that the church is not primarily about the leader of a church, but about the people in a church. For a minister's family, this means we learn how to adapt to new places, quickly and often. I paid close attention as a child to the unwritten local rules governing how to get by and, if lucky, the implicit guidelines for how to make friends. I tried to do this fast, knowing I might only be in one school for a year. My earliest memories are about moving, not about staying put.

I am now a scholar and teacher at what is called a "Tier One" university. One explicit rule of success at a leading university for young leaders is to act always like you are a floating free agent. A scholar fit to be at a fancy-pants, cosmopolitan university is to be ready, even eager, to move herself and her family for a better offer elsewhere. I have been at Duke University for almost seventeen years. For a decade I tried to pretend that I was that sort of free agent scholar. I failed. I love Durham, North Carolina, the city where Duke sits, and I wanted to raise my daughters here. I lost any game of poker I tried to play with my boss here or with bosses at other institutions, because I do not have a player's soul or a poker face. Try as I might to appear rootless, I am rooted here.

About five years ago, I stopped trying to play poker. I embraced my calling to be a scholar, publicly, right here in one place. The REM song "Stand" ran in my mental jukebox, and I played it on my phone while hula-hooping in my backyard. God used songwriter Michael Stipe's words to help me recover my balance. Turning north. Turning south. Remembering where I am and why I am here. I received my bearings.

Once a month for over two years I have written missives of love to my neighbors in my home state. Standing in the place where I live, I have tried to use the best charism I have at my disposal—my writing—to invite conversation in churches and coffee shops and around dinner tables. The responses I have received, in person and in writing, have taught me how to be a locally accountable, political theologian. I have tried in this way to put the practical back into practical theology, practicing it in print for people who live in Durham.

Local papers across the United States are hanging on by a thin line of wire, and the *Durham Herald-Sun* is no different. Those of us who read and write for local papers believe that a popular bumper sticker needs to be revised to read "Think Locally and Read Locally." Ten years ago the bumper sticker I read again and again in Durham was "Think Local; Act Global." My missives of love are not a vow against "globalism," whatever precisely "globalism" means, but a commitment to stand where we are and find out more about where the heck we actually are in each local region.

Local papers can be a crucial part of a flourishing city or town, not only informing people of goings-on, but also uncovering rocks carefully used by some to keep secret goings-on secret to all but a few. Local journalism can also be a hedge against meaningless cosmopolitanism. The person who taught me this first is a Quaker friend who grew up in North Carolina. She explained that cosmopolitanism is tempting for people who want to appear in the know. It is an alluring trap, where your identity is forged primarily as a cool person of the world who knows how to quote the latest BBC miniseries, the most recent journal of this or that political avant-garde, or the winningest soccer team.

There has been a turn in towns like Portland and Durham and Austin to make "local" itself a marker of cool. But localism is also a privilege. Some people may be logistically stuck in a locale where they cannot feasibly escape, wanting to leave the town where they currently sleep but unable to pool the resources to move their family somewhere else. "Localism" as a marker of cool also assumes you do not have to jump the next train car to pick the next crop coming to season elsewhere. Many working people have to itinerate for all sorts of horrible, economically brutal reasons. Writing locally also assumes the time to write at all, and publishing locally requires someone willing to put your words to a page as worth someone's read.

Standing where I am, able by the kindness of others, sheer luck, and a complicated version of grace to remain here, I offer these letters. I hope they inspire you, as you are able, to learn about your own place, and to visit with your neighbors about how to flourish and fight well together. These essays are in part about the hard work of working together with people you do not know otherwise for the sake of better paychecks, roads, schools, parks, healthcare, grocery stores—all of the politically hard-won basics that make up that elusive gift some theologians call "community."

These essays are also, therefore, my way of protesting a political turn within Christianity toward asceticism, austerity, humility, and obedience. The powers that be institutionalized in many regions across the US (and the UK) offer a political theology with advice to the leading leaders about how to be more responsible with their power. In these essays, I tacitly (and at times explicitly) ask for neighbors to reject austerity and obedience. I suggest that people be proud, fight hard for local beauty, and be strategically disobedient together. I assume I am not writing for leaders, but for other people who want change.

The opinion essays are sometimes explicitly Christian, but not always. For readers who want to know how I speak when talking straight-up about Jesus, I have included three sermons. These sermons were given to people who had gathered in a room designated specifically for Christian worship. If that is your preference, you may want to begin at the end of this book. I have tried to weave the gospel through all of the essays, however, in ways that will be useful politically and personally for my neighbors of faith and my neighbors who think faith itself is the primary problem.

This was my first essay for the *Durham Herald-Sun*. I had no idea whether it was good or not. I had broken all the rules that university advisors and political lobbyists had given me for writing a "successful" opinion essay. It really did begin just as I wrote it, as a mom trying to sort out local nonsense with my school-age daughters. Many of the essays afterward follow the same pattern: being a mom, trying to parent well, trying to make my corner of the world a little better for children like my daughters and mothers like me.

GOODBYE TAX FREE WEEKEND

August, 2013

"Huh? This is the last tax free weekend for school stuff?" my daughter asked this morning, "I thought the guys in charge were *against* taxes? Why would they cancel our weekend without taxes?" We do live in confusing times.

Getting ready for tax holiday weekend has been a ritual for my girls. We've made a wish list in addition to the must list for back to school. The official supply roster arrives in the mail the week before, and we clear several hours to bargain shop. The plan includes not only the basics—spirals, pencils, the (increasingly complicated and expensive) calculator for math class—but also a few new outfits. On my youngest daughter's list this year is a trendy, asymmetrical skirt, longer in the back than the front. She's aged out of sneakers that sparkle as she steps, and is entering the world of tween moxie. Now, I realize that a brand-new outfit is not strictly necessary. Unlike the pink eraser and bottle of glue, that skirt is not essential. But shopping for fashion whimsy is a way we've celebrated the gift of a new year together. The amount we save on tax free weekend contributes not only dollars and cents to our home budget, but to our sense that the men and women who make our laws have such details of life in mind.

The same goes for ballet and tap shoes, baseball gloves, shin guards, and ice skates—a few of the things on the North Carolina tax exempt holiday weekend list under "recreational equipment." Recreation is not technically, absolutely crucial for the basic, daily survival of children and teenagers, but the word "recreation" itself puts the matter well. Football, ballet, and ice skating are, at their best, re-creating and revitalizing for individual children, and for families and neighborhoods across this state. North Carolina's tax-exempt weekend has been a concrete way to note that recreation is good for actual children we know, and that stuff like special shoes and gloves and guards make up the rhythm of a yearly sports season. It has been a way for lawmakers to show everyone that they do know a fact of a flourishing state: we don't thrive on math alone.

Of course, a few of my mom friends have assiduously avoided tax free weekend. They are cushioned from the harshest effects of the current economy, and the extra dollars saved seem not worth the extra time cheek to cheek in the checkout line. But the tax holiday has had a different feel from the squish-or-be-squished Friday after Thanksgiving frenzy. It has been a chance for me to meet children and parents while picking out a lunch box or trying out awkward new soccer cleats. It has been an annual way for people in my little corner of North Carolina to acknowledge together that we are cutting coupons and pinching pennies to buy the bits and pieces that make up a school year, because the children in our homes and schools and neighborhoods matter.

The legislators who voted to drop North Carolina's tax free weekend missed out on a simple way to show they understand how actual parents of real boys and girls across our state budget and bond. It is their loss, and ours.

P.S. The editor liked this essay enough to publish it! He invited me to breakfast and asked me to write a monthly column for the paper. I was overjoyed, but also intimidated. What if I could not do this twice? I took inspiration from my many friends and former students who preach every Sunday, every week. Somehow I would find something worth 800 words once a month. I did receive feedback from readers on this one. I am what we used to call in Texas a "yellow-dog Democrat," meaning that I would vote for a yellow dog if she were on the ballot. But even

Republican friends wrote me to note that the current North Carolina legislature is being run by people who do not seem to have one clue about how real, working people live in North Carolina. Because Republican friends had found this essay helpful, I tried, in many of these essays, to be both honest and persuasive. I have pulled a few punches, so to speak, in order to try to reach local readers who might otherwise dismiss me as a hopelessly naïve liberal.

This is an obvious follow-up to the previous essay, but it has a backstory. These essays are sometimes like stringing beads on a necklace. I want to pull in readers who liked the last entry, and also pull them toward another question in Durham or in the state of North Carolina that they might not have considered before. So, I begin here nearly where I left off in the last entry, with a new word about the importance of desegregation in Durham.

BACK TO SCHOOL

September, 2013

"They paved the entrance!" My older daughter and I were at Riverside High early, sorting her schedule, and she was touched by this simple thing. Like locking doors on the bathroom stalls, a library catalogue system, or a tuned piano, that smooth asphalt showed that someone allocating money cares about Riverside. She is a senior this year, with one wing already out of the nest. My baby started at Lakewood Middle on Monday, anticipating her first locker. This has been a week to have a dream, and I am unabashedly wishing for lots more money for our public schools.

I moved to Durham fourteen years ago, and I did not give schools a second thought. Both of my daughters' grandmothers retired from public school teaching in Texas, and choosing differently would have seemed as traitorous to my parents as buying a foreign-made car would have seemed to theirs. I could not initially interpret the awkwardness around the school question. I eventually realized that people's anxiety was not about salaries for teachers and such, matters I'd been taught to worry over. Friends were concerned about race. One with a daughter who looks like mine explained she was concerned about "experimentation." She did not mean studies conducted on kids in a region replete with social scientists. She was worried her daughter would crisscross the color line.

It took years of legal wrangling to integrate Durham's children. One photo from that era is as iconic in Durham as Norman

Rockwell's "The Problem We All Live With." In the 1959 picture, Floyd and Evelyn McKissick escort their daughter Andree and Henry Vickers to attend the previously all-white Carr Junior High. I've heard stories about the African American children who were trailblazers in Durham, and they had to practice composure beyond reckoning. For my own girls, the most pointed question they faced each new elementary year was whether they "go for" UNC or Duke. The question of the desegregation era was "the NAACP versus the KKK," as one trailblazer put it. His mere presence at the school signaled not only his allegiance, but his role as a free-throw shooter for the opposing team.

Around 1922, the city of Durham had budgeted $325,000 to build Durham High School (white) and $125,000 for Hillside High School (black). Almost 50 years later, the city redrew zoning, and Hillside, a remarkably successful black school, integrated. For some white teenagers, it seemed like their world had shifted "overnight." Jean (Rogers) Flowers related how this felt. "My parents told me: 'This is where we live, and the plan says you're going to Hillside, so we're going to try it.'" She continued, "It was a beautiful time, but we were so green. I was disappointed not to be with my girlfriends, but, in retrospect, it may have been good that cliques were broken apart." Jean began to crisscross the divide. She had been a cheerleader, and principal John Harding Lucas encouraged her to "go out" for the squad. "I had learned a cheering style that was stiff and jilted," she laughed, "and I didn't know if I could learn a different style, but to this day I prefer rhythm and blues." Lucas taught them to stitch friendships along the 20 percent–80 percent racial seam, and her French teacher, Mrs. Christopher, organized her interracial class to fundraise for a trip to France. "Over time, we grew to be *not* scared of each other. I prefer to be on a road where I know what's ahead, and we didn't know," Jean said. She now counts this uncertainty a blessing.

The movie about a 1971 integrated football team, *Remember the Titans*, is a favorite. It reminds Jean of her *alma mater*. Roger Ebert wrote of that movie, "Real life is never this simple, but then that's what the movies are for." Which brings me back to my dream.

What Jean described is close to kinship. The Latin phrase "alma mater" means, after all, "nourishing mother." Jean learned how to cheer differently, and she learned to root for a new team.

Today, with cut after cut to public schools, parents are set up to argue over a smaller and smaller slice of money pie—a strategy designed to divide and conquer. I counter division with a dream— a dream of a Durham where little black boys and black girls will be able to join hands with little white boys and white girls as sisters and brothers. I am dreaming of a Durham where black boys and white girls figure out their lockers together, and save up for a school trip, and savor ample classroom space and their teacher's attentive time, discovering their individually unique gifts alongside one another. Some people making decisions seem scared of this dream. Why?

P.S. There is a proposal on the table in Durham to create an all-boys, all minority charter school. Several women in the school system have been critical of this initiative, a nd have come under scrutiny from a few prominent African-American pastors in Durham. This continues to be a hotly contested question in Durham. Truthfully, I was ginger-footed with this essay. I wanted to write at the end that the charter school plan is bad, misguided, and even backward. But I left it open for readers to make that connection themselves. I am not sure it was the right decision. Durham has fissures that cross every possible division—racial, economic, and familial—and any initiative has a backstory. I will summon up the courage to write more on this in the future. You will read intimations of these issues in the essays to come. Recently, the radio show *This American Life* ran a story on public schools, and how the best formula for pedagogy includes schools that are mixed in every way. My suspicion is that divided schools are the promoted answer because childhood solidarity is a truly potent recipe for, well . . . solidarity. Catechesis starts early in churches for a reason. As that song about racism goes in the musical *South Pacific*: "You've got to be carefully taught! Before it's too late! Before you are six, or seven, or eight!" If children are taught early that they can be friends across the divisions that otherwise divide neighbor from neighbor, they might refuse the carefully taught lessons of division.

Duke Divinity School's Youth Academy had a dress code, and there is an implicit dress code at Duke Divinity for worship teams. Recently there was even an explicit dress code—a very conservative one—for the praise choir at my workplace. And, every mother wants to be thought of as the sort of mother who would encourage her daughters to dress modestly, right? But, no, I have learned the hard way that modesty is overrated, and that adolescent girls should not be taught that their bodies are sites for danger or shame. There is courage between the lines of this essay on leggings.

ON LEGGINGS AND LEADERSHIP

October, 2013

My dad is a Methodist minister, and, the summer I turned twelve, our bishop moved us from Austin to San Angelo, a town straight out of *Friday Night Lights*. I now wax poetic about the stark beauty of West Texas. Then, it seemed like Mars. I had to learn to make friends on this new planet, and that involved figuring out the un-written dress code for adolescent success. In the preppy era, the basic outfit would be Calvin Klein jeans and an Izod top. But in 1980 a brand of jeans called "Luv-it" was in vogue. These came with designs embroidered on the back pocket—rainbows, horses, hearts, lipstick, cookies, and words like "foxy." My own favorite featured a yellow rose. Optimally, you owned five pair, a different design for each day of the week. This was an expensive fad, and I booked every babysitting job I could get. But I relished every purchase. With differently embellished pockets on my backside, I forged my identity and figured out ways to fit in.

When picking up my oldest from high school in Durham, I have marveled at the carnival of fashion. There is no "Preppy Handbook" ruling over this generation. There are mohawk hair-cuts in different colors, braids with shell beads, a twelve-gored jean skirt with carefully frayed edges alongside a plaid a-line skirt from Talbots. I am sure there are subtleties of snobbery going on, but what I notice from this distance is how imaginative my daughter's friends are.

Her sister is now in sixth grade, seeking a signature style. The three of us had a confusing conversation recently about the DPS handbook rules on clothing. "No yoga pants," she insisted. "What's wrong with yoga?" I asked. (*I* merely endure yoga, but I was pretty sure no one had outlawed it yet.) My older daughter explained that the rule against leggings has been extended to yoga pants. "It's about booties, Mom." Turns out, the rule is about obscuring the particular contours of a girl's backside. "But haven't you worn yoga pants to school?" I asked my eldest. "Has anyone tried to send you home?" "Mom," she rolled her eyes at my color-blind cluelessness, "I won't get sent home; I'm not black." Wow. Yoga pants, like leggings, have ample leg coverage, usually from waist to ankle, and, unlike blue jeans, they allow a nice freedom of movement. They are comfy. I have worn my favorite pair to Sunday worship at Trinity UMC, so I can slip out afterward to yoga class. But they don't "leave much to the imagination," as my father would say. Apparently some adults are afraid the sight will distract during algebra.

I mentioned this rule to my graduate students, and one of them sent me an article on what appears to be a national trend for public school reform in "ethnically and economically diverse" school districts. Nancy L. Cohen lives in Los Angeles, and the title of her piece for the *Guardian* website reads: "Welcome back to school, girls. And mind those breasts!" She laments: "My daughters' school has a new dress code: No bellies. No buns. No breasts." One of my Duke classes had a frank conversation about how far administrators should go in their quest for uniformity and focus. A woman in the class who grew up near the equator noted that everyone in her school wore as little as possible due to the heat. "Somehow, funny enough, we learned plenty, even with lots of skin showing."

What about hair? Growing up in Texas, there wasn't only the difficulty of fickle hair trends. There were also rules about boys and hair length, and ear piercings. One friend tried styling himself like the androgynous MTV star Adam Ant. He not only got the snot beaten out of him by some other boys, but he was called into the principal's office and scolded. Today, I am grateful my daughters have friends who adopt and adapt different styles of self-expression and claim their individuality, whether that means combing the sales racks at Nordstrom's, spending their few work-free hours picking through thrift shops, or making screen-printed T-shirts. And I hope for both the girls and boys a sense that their bodies are not treacherous distractions but beautiful gifts from a good creator.

I think there are lots of ways in this world to be distracted from proper focus. Underfunded and overworked public school administrators in cities like Durham are being pushed and pulled in various directions by educational snake-oil salesmen intent to sell cheap and/or trendy solutions to real problems facing kids and their families during this grisly recession. I don't think blurring my daughter's backside or regulating your son's hair is the solution. We are capable of more creative leadership than that.

P.S. Some of the children at my daughter's school led a subversive "Leggings Tuesday." Kids had been encouraging both boys and girls to wear leggings to school. Parents across the school received phone calls one night from the principal, telling us in no uncertain terms that anyone wearing leggings to school would be sent home. I worried that somehow I had inadvertently started this, not by my op-ed, which had appeared in the paper over a year before this "Leggings Tuesday," but by my work with undergraduates at Duke. I had been teaching a first-year seminar with sixty students. Faculty team-teaching the course had been asked to talk informally about our work one evening. I allowed students to ask me any question they had for me as an "ethicist" or as a "mother" or as a "woman scholar." One of the young women asked me what I later called the Miss America question. If I could do one thing in the world what would it be? I told the group that I would abolish dress codes across Durham. I do not dream of changing the world, but I do dream of waving a magic wand and changing some nonsense in my own locale. When I explained to the Duke undergraduates the dress code and why I thought it was unhealthy for girls, many of them came up with the idea of a "Leggings" day, where everyone would wear leggings to protest the code. Duke undergraduates regularly tutor in Durham Public Schools. The call from the principal at my daughter's school came only a few weeks after this interview with Duke undergraduates. I am not sure I prompted the kerfuffle. But I like to think I helped. The fastest growing network of evangelical churches in Durham have as their spokesman an aesthetically normative, weight-lifting hunk, who wears blue jeans that fit him like Captain America's tights. So, are leggings in public schools really a menace to order? I submit not.

Writing these essays helped me to be attuned to the basic assumptions of life in North Carolina. One is the state fair. Friends who work in nail and beauty salons have told me that the month of October is slow, because people are spending their expendable income going to the fair, eating fair food, and attending concerts related to the fair. The North Carolina State Fair is a fascinating cross-section of a region, even more so than Disney World or Six Flags over Texas. The State Fair of North Carolina brings together people who otherwise do not shop in the same grocery stores and certainly do not worship in the same spaces. It brings together people who would never stop at a truck stop to use the restroom and people who rely on truck stops for hospitality when on long road trips. It is a vision of heaven.

FITTER FAMILIES?

November, 2013

I have lived in North Carolina since the summer of 1999, but I had never been to the state fair. I finally took a posse of girls last Saturday. We ate too much, and we spent too much money playing games you can't win. But my youngest daughter has a keen shooting eye, it turns out. She won a giant, plush duck at a water pistol gallery. I fooled one of the "guess your age" guys by thirteen years and won a little duck, along with a ridiculously self-satisfied smirk, which I wore for several days. We had as much fun talking with strangers in the queue for the hurl-a-whirl as we did on the actual ride itself. The state fair is a giant slice of North Carolina humanity, and we didn't have to pay extra for the fantastic variety of home. Fried Oreos, the best free hush puppies on the planet, black coffee from the friendly kids at the Future Farmers of America booth . . . to borrow an English idiom, it is all part of life's rich pageant.

When my grandmother was a little girl, state fairs didn't have multiple rides named "Vortex" or competing, synthesized dance music coming from large stereos, and I don't think you had to wash up with antimicrobial soap after petting the world's biggest hog. It was a simpler time, maybe. But fairs in those days had one feature I am glad we've lost. For decades in the first half of the twentieth century, good Christian citizens across the heartland walked into buildings marked "Fitter Families for Future Firesides" and had themselves tested for eugenic fitness. Families judged worthy of a B+ or higher received medals that declared "Yea I have a goodly heritage." My grandmother's generation may have been better able than today's to recognize the "goodly heritage" phrase as biblical (Ps 16), but many Christians at the time didn't protest this misapplication. The Psalm sings praises to God, who alone secures goodness. The "Fitter Family" medal featured two distinctly Aryan parents pouring out symbolic goodness to their lone toddler, who stands apart, with upturned hands.

North Carolina's grim history of forced or coerced sterilization is part of a larger story. And don't let anyone tell you the story is solely southern. The pattern of eugenics in our state is marked by intricate, distinctly southern fissures, but the summons to breed better families was popularized across the US, preached in mainline Protestant pulpits, and advocated in distinguished halls of learning from New Haven, Connecticut to Stanford, California. One of the reasons I worked so hard with my publisher to secure the Norman Rockwell image on the cover of my second book, a book about parenthood, is that I wanted from the very beginning to signal that eugenics was neither idiosyncratic nor foreign. Eugenics was as American as the state fair, apple pie, and Norman Rockwell (an artist I readily confess to loving). Some of the "best and brightest" Americans of Rockwell's generation used their unique gifts to persuade people like my grandmother to internalize a sense of her responsibility to select a genetically fit mate, to choose genetically fit friends, and to teach standards of eugenic fitness to children in their public and Sunday school classrooms. By submitting themselves and their children to new, standardized intelligence and physical testing of various sorts, aspiring, mainstream Americans sought to prove their "goodly heritage." They were tricked to trade an inheritance of free grace for a mess of self-justifying porridge.

Why learn history if you can't help but just keep repeating the mistakes? Here are two lessons I learned while researching eugenics. First, the key men who were the grand strategists of the movement in the US saw themselves as engaged in holy husbandry. They viewed actual, individual human beings as examples of larger, population-wide problems or patterns. They sought to comprehend and shape real people like you and me from the vantage point of a higher being, with a higher calling than merely mortal love. As a farmer might dispassionately choose which chickens to breed and which to isolate, these men wanted to manage human beings on a large scale, overseeing from above the advancement of the race. Second, eugenic propaganda trained everyday people to internalize this way of being seen. Teachers, farmers, and small business owners were encouraged to see themselves and their children as akin to nonhuman livestock in a large-scale agribusiness. Eugenics was a concerted effort to teach people to assess themselves and their neighbors critically, and to accept the concept that each life requires proof of fitness for citizenry. It was a good way to separate neighbor from neighbor, and to divide a person from within, under a banner of progress.

P.S. A much older friend at my church had told me years ago that he had been involved in the North Carolina sterilization project. This project lasted into the 1970s, and the state government finally acknowledged the extensive work of local and state boards in sterilizing women deemed by authorities to be a drain on the local economy. The quest for a "New South," able to attract new industries like those that crisscross Alabama and Mississippi, required both labor laws that effectively prohibited the unionization of industrial workers, but also ways to shift perceptions of the South as genetically retrograde. While individual members of local sterilization boards possibly believed they were indeed lessening human suffering by coerced or forced sterilization, they were working within a framework of progressive politics that continues to this day. Conversations about public schools and children or youth with special needs is just one example where public discussions treat individual children of God as factors in a wheel of economic gain or loss. I hoped that this essay would prompt conversations across generations about the time when this coarse reckoning was, well . . . coarse, and to allow people to think about how neighbors still evaluate neighbors as worthy recipients of basic public expenditures that make life livable together. So, the populist cacophony of the state fair prompted me to write a piece again about solidarity. It is a summons to see our history with sobriety and find another way toward what I will daringly call love.

Bullying continues to be a topic of conversation for parents, children, teachers, and women who are asked to comment about anything related to parenting, children, teaching, and mothering. "Bullying" is not a topic of conversation among CEOs or middle management in segments of the workplaces dominated by men. "Bullying" is a school yard problem, a problem for mothers, a problem for nannies. I have been a girl on a schoolyard, a mother, and a nanny. I learned early on to see how people, young and old, are bullied by peers and people with power to determine how they endure their day of schoolwork, or work.

BULLIES

December, 2013

One of the most asinine things I have ever heard on the radio was from a sports news commentator, who said recently that it was ridiculous to think that an NFL football player could be "bullied." Presumably, due to their size and strength, large men who routinely endure the impact of a refrigerator to their heads cannot be fazed by someone trying, through words, to mess with their heads. As a West Texas girl, I know football, and, as a female professor at an elite university, I know men. Men are definitely capable of bullying and being bullied, regardless of how much weight they can bench press or how many fancy degrees they have. It has to do in part with their being men.

A very wise, older bishop commented about one manager we both worked with that he'd never seen a man so effective at emasculating other men. It was this manager's modus operandi: control through emasculation. You can't emasculate a woman— that is, make her feel like a woman. A woman is a woman, and, while you can bully women in all sorts of miserably effective ways, you can't bully a woman by accusing her of being a woman. A tried and true way to bully a man is to call him feminine. A common epithet to use on a man is a derogatory term for a part of a woman that designates her as female. (The word is a synonym for kitten.)

Grown men can be intimidated to toe the team line by creating a context where they are afraid of being shamed in front of others as less than fully masculine. I've seen truly gifted, creative faculty colleagues wither under the subtle hazing of an administration that consistently labels their research "weak" or their writing style "shrill" or their scholarly output "small." A boy growing up in the US is carefully taught through a chorus of loud and quiet cues that he is supposed to be strong (not weak), that his developed voice is to be low (not shrill), and that the size of his body or some other measurable extension of his ego is to be large. Some men don't so much wither as harden in such a context, putting up a shell of stoicism and even keeping their distance from anyone vaguely vulnerable or anyone actually female. But stoicism requires, for most human beings, expending mental energy that would be so much better spent on other things. Bullying through emasculation is bad sportsmanship and bad management in part because, while it may elicit compliance, it squishes any spirit of creativity. It also rots true camaraderie from the core. Within such a system, men sense that their dignity is precarious, as their teammates or coworkers may be asked to turn on them.

A few football players I know were kind enough to talk to me about the recent bullying story concerning the Miami Dolphins, and one expressed dismay that the young man had kept such a long silence about the abuse he allegedly endured. Maybe his silence was in part about shame. In my experience as a teacher and as a pastor, I have learned that women or men who have endured abuse for any length of time are often embarrassed. It can be excruciating to go into detail about a pattern of prolonged bullying, enduring people's well-meaning questions or incredulity. I also know that it can be a tricky business pointing out to male co-workers that their conformity may be due to strategic bullying. Men don't necessarily appreciate being shown how they are being subtly controlled by men (or women) managing them. Rules about what makes a real man a real man intensify the pressure to pretend that nothing is happening.

While domination through shame may seep like a poison through a team or an organization, courage can also be contagious. A key question I learned to ask in community organizing is this: "Tell us a story about when you stood up for yourself." Sharing stories about hard-won courage in a workplace can help break the spell of stoicism or acquiescence. Here is a story from Texas football. My dad's middle school team was the Palo Pinto Possums. The girls had outnumbered the boys in the vote for mascot. To be fair to the girls, possums are fierce, in their own little way. But a possum's best-known defense is to roll over and play dead. My dad says those boys played the best football of any team, they were so determined to reclaim the humble possum for grandeur. It is possible for boys and men to refuse to be divided and conquered through tactical emasculation. Heck, these days, it is even possible for a few girls to make the team.

P.S. One of the last essays in this book involves my attempt to blow a whistle about how money was distributed at Duke University during a time of supposedly obligatory austerity. I helped to organize a series of three street theaters to draw attention to the way that people who work at Duke were being subtly bullied, while some executives at Duke were blithely accumulating very large bonuses for themselves and their families. This essay helped me to name ways that I had seen bullying in my own workplace. It also helped me to think about how best to explain to people who asked that I had heard many stories about domination in North Carolina. One of the congregations that asked me to speak to them early in my time at Duke, around 1999–2000, was a quite prestigious congregation with solid roots in the aristocracy of North Carolina. I spoke to a room of 200 people or so, on how Saint Augustine, a fifth-century writer, had taught people that lying is so very dangerous because it is a use of a human capacity that splits the soul. Lying is an act of using our beautiful, God-given brains and our precious, God-crafted tongues to say something that we do not believe. Bullying is a way to intimidate children or adults to use our lives to say something other than what we know to be true. I have heard, in testimony after testimony, that bullying is a problem for octogenarians and football players and pharmacists and researchers and, yes, for school children too. The way I have learned to resist bullying is by asking friends to help. Which, of course, requires me to find and to trust people who will see the intricate dynamics of destructive power among people. I trust daily that God is stronger than the bully that my Baptist grandmother would name clearly as the Prince of Evil.

Christmas caught me by surprise in 2013. I was having a complicated relationship with Christmas, because it had been, for a very
long time, a season of painful pretend. Christmas can be a time of
cruel nostalgia—of encouraging people, usually women, to rec-
reate some past version of Christmas that a parent or grandpar-
ent had hoisted onto an extended family. I risked sentimentality.

ON THE TWELFTH DAY OF CHRISTMAS

January, 2014

I know. Most people are sick of Christmas by now. The snowmen
appeared at the mall like fat, tardy ghosts a day after Halloween.
But I am a sucker for Christmas anything and everything. I am like
Auntie Mame belting out "Yes, we need a little Christmas! Right
this very minute!" Even in March. I caught the bug from my mom,
who has her Christmas tree up all year. She changes the decorations
to fit the closest holiday. There's a Groundhog Christmas tree, then
a Valentine's Christmas tree, a Shamrock Christmas tree, a Fourth
of July Christmas tree . . . maybe it is because her birthday falls a
week before Christmas, and her name is Carol. I was conditioned
early to savor Christmas details like snowflakes in a barren land.

But I didn't inherit either sappy Christmas sentimentalism
or Christian jingly jingoism, thank the stars. First, my mom had
a rule about sermons that covers lots of bases regarding holiday
stories. No tales of dying children allowed in a sermon. Charles
Dickens gets away with it, with the Tiny Tim versus Scrooge shtick.
But your average preacher can't. For one thing, there are children
sitting in the pews, and they don't need yet another reason to be
anxious. For another, a dying child story in a sermon is invariably
a last-ditch, cheap effort to make people *feel* something, because
too many of us think that Christianity is about *feeling* something.
Regarding jingly jingoism, where I grew up, no Christians I knew
were embattled and defensive about Christmas. After all, the one
Jewish kid in my graduating class had to get permission each year

to miss school on his family's holiest days. We got Christmas week off for free, as if a break around December 25 were as natural as the sun rising in the east. The way I was brought up, that wasn't warrant to gloat.

I had a delightfully improbable exchange about sap and jingoism with a woman at the checkout counter in a Cracker Barrel in Arkansas last week. I was trying on some of their charming snowflake hats, and we started chatting in that lively, kindred-spirit way that some women do, mostly about how much we both adore Christmas kitsch. She then told me and several other customers that she was really determined to keep talking to everybody about Jesus, because "they" are trying to keep her from "talking about Jesus." "Who is 'they'? Your managers?" I whispered, conspiratorially. "Oh, not at all. You know, just *them!*" she said, with a wave of her hand. Without really thinking, I said that I thought the word that could really get a woman in trouble these days is the v-word (an anatomical phrase which, yes, I actually said out loud) and then told her about the Michigan State Representative who was barred from speaking on the house floor back in June for saying the v-word. To the dismay of several men standing around, she and I both then sorted out together that Jesus himself must not have been too scared of the v-word, given that, for heaven's sake, didn't he come out of one?

And this brings me to the finest cinematic representation of Christmas ever crafted. I am speaking, of course, about the denouement of the Peanuts Trilogy (1965–1973). Linus van Pelt's recitation of the Gospel of Luke served for several generations as *the* Christmas story. We had watched Linus at Halloween, tenaciously holding out hope that sincerity ("without a hint of hypocrisy") is rewarded. The pumpkin patch he had chosen was perfect because there was "nothing but sincerity as far as the eye can see." We had watched his big sister Lucy resolutely leave her warm bed to fetch Linus home, having set her alarm to 4:00 AM. And, after the 1973 Thanksgiving special aired, the trilogy included Peppermint Patty's inimitable kismet, as she stumbles a group of friends into an invitation to turkey dinner at Charlie Brown's grandmother's condominium. As the kids in the back of the station wagon sing "Over the River and Through the Woods" off key and off beat, my family knew they had a clue about us. By the Christmas special, as Charlie Brown confesses to Linus that he "doesn't feel the way [he's] supposed to feel" at Christmas, and that he always ends up "depressed," I knew someone understood that the holiday trifecta of candy, kin, and faith that is Halloween to Thanksgiving to Christmas is difficult, and that Christmas isn't about the correct feeling, or the faultless meal, or the careful configuration of invited friends. It is about anticipating God's goodness, in spite of us and right here with us, in a sign—a baby, born for peace.

P.S. I cannot say going through a breaking and then broken marriage has been a blessing. It was not a blessing, and I would not wish such misery on my worst enemy. But God has given me opened eyes to see that holidays are hard for people who have suffered loss.

The woman who inspired this essay is Professor Helen F. (Sunny) Ladd.

UNBROKEN

February, 2014

"I don't want to hear the words 'broken schools' one more time!" This senior scholar of education usually speaks with the tone of a high school physics teacher—measured, clear, and calm. But she is fed up. We were at a forum on North Carolina women and politics recently, and a young woman had just used the phrase to ask a reasonable question about child-to-teacher ratios. This scholar responded by sternly warning us not to buy into the jargon of "brokenness." Since her uncharacteristic rant, those two words have jangled in my ears when I hear them. She made them as jarring to my teacher sensibility as a split infinitive. "Broken schools." I now contend that this phrase has been part of a smart scheme to set up the terms for a conversation about who can come in and "fix" education across the country. "Broken?" Think about it. Is that the right word for the man who mopped up vomit when a second-grader overindulged in Halloween candy? Or the woman who remembered my daughter's cafeteria account number when her little fourth grade mind was otherwise engaged, busy wiggling her newly loose tooth? Or the cop at the high school who has to deal with one more confounded fender bender resulting from teens "checking one another out" rather than carefully backing out? To borrow from a cute pop song, the public school system's "not broken, just bent." The question we ought to ask is this: who bent it?

The example of sneaky old Mr. Potter from *It's a Wonderful Life* is useful. If you want effectively to undermine the complicated, daily work of teachers and custodians and counselors and school traffic cops, you first need to destabilize people's confidence in the solvency of the overall system. You basically need to create the educational equivalent of a run on the bank. People are hearing through grapevines as disparate as National Public Radio and Fox News that public schools are "broken" and in need of a superhero leader-ish leader to come in and rescue them. So, we become susceptible to the idea that there is a kind of broad, cultural consensus that public education is failing. Polls can be made to say almost anything, but it seems that most parents with children in public schools carry in their brains, simultaneously, two divergent things. First, they basically appreciate the people who are caring for their children and think they ought to make more money and have job security. But, second, they think there is a broad consensus that public schools are "broken." Similarly, in *It's a Wonderful Life*, people in the town genuinely love George Bailey, his uncle Bill Bailey, and his cousin Tilly, who together (with a crow) manage the local Building and Loan Association with fairness and finesse. But anxiety can be as contagious as courage, and Old Man Potter takes advantage of people's fear to divide them and turn them against the Building and Loan. A crucial turning point in the story comes when the frantic citizens look around and see one another rightly, again, for what they are—neighbors—buying into a future, for a town they truly hold together.

As anyone who has a television knows, Uncle Billy haphazardly misplaces a huge pile of cash held in trust, and Mr. Potter, by chance, wins the opportunity to hoard it and wreak havoc. In the case of North Carolina, as in other states, various versions of Old Man Potter have quite intentionally underfunded the public school system. For example, they've cut the penny sales tax as well as the godzillionaire tax. And then they've had the gall to fake avuncular concern that our underfunded public schools are not serving children well, participating in events funded by corporate sponsors to showcase "school choice." North Carolina now pays our public school teachers less than in forty-six other states. We are now forty-sixth in the country. That shouldn't scare us. That should make us mad. As Deborah R. Gerhardt reported in *Slate* a few weeks ago, "North Carolina public schools would have to hire 29,300 people to get back up to the employee-per-student ratio the schools had in 2008." Voters who can read well, and who can read between the lines, are not easily manipulated. Maybe this is a reason why the Potters of our beautiful state are trying to send us running scared, ready to yank our children out from under the tutelage and care of hardworking and good-hearted people we actually know and trust. It is a crucial time in our own little story, a time to look around and see one another for who we are—neighbors, together in this endeavor of public education, for the long haul and for our children's good.

P.S. My mother is a public school teacher. She was also a Methodist minister's wife, itinerating wherever my dad was called. I am an educator, and I was raised by a public school teacher. When I first saw the movie *Norma Rae*, I knew who Sally Field reminded me of. The workplace was different, but the moxie was familiar. My mom is 4' 9" and weighed about 100 pounds wet. She followed my dad for his work, and she had to start over repeatedly. She had to clamber up from the bottom of the isolated systems that were public school districts in Texas at that time. These systems were often uniquely absurdist, overseen by people who may or may not have been gifted by God for administration. I say "uniquely" absurdist because each school system, whether overseen by a gifted or inept administrator, had people lower in the system trying to curry favor and aver disfavor from the particular man in charge in our "right to hire and fire" state. When the *pater familias* has free rein, the people below him have to figure out the explicit or opaque rules of the particular game. My mom had to figure out how to secure and keep her job, again and again and again, under a new set of rules in a new context, while teaching whatever the school system had need for at the time. She is a genius, and she has the pluck of Crystal Lee Sutton (the real Norma Rae) so she was somehow able still to love teaching junior and senior high for three decades and also truly to befriend, love, support, and encourage the teachers around her. But my mom always wanted and needed a teachers' union. I need a labor union just as much as my mom did. Universities are as pressurized by funding stresses and small fiefdoms as any other institution or corporation in the United States today. I need a working coalition of educators who support one another to pursue our gifts of teaching, writing, and research with dignity and the freedom to write without fear of reprisal. I need the power of collective bargaining, so we see one another as co-workers and not competitors. And I need the tools to organize, so we can work together and secure the best working place for our students and ourselves. It was around the time I published this essay that the AFL-CIO in North Carolina asked me to help connect labor unions with congregations, in an effort called "Labor Sabbath" that you can find online.

Sometimes I am not certain that a concern is idiosyncratically my own, or is a legitimate focus for an essay. I was not sure that camera surveillance was a widespread problem until I mentioned that I was working on this essay to a gathering of women. We were rehearsing for a campus-wide production of *The Vagina Monologues*, and several of the women talked about cameras in their own workplaces—hospitals, schools, shops—and how they felt under scrutiny in ways that were hindering, not enhancing, their interactions with the people they were to care for and serve. Performing on a stage, saying the word "vagina" in front of hundreds of people, I was gaining my courage to name more clearly to myself that my writing is both personal and political, in ways that are legitimately public.

UP WITH PEOPLE, DOWN WITH SURVEILLANCE

March, 2014

I have been shaking my fist on the way to church on Sunday mornings. I am more prone to dance in the car (much to my daughters' embarrassment) than to shake my fist, but I admit to fist shaking at certain lights between my house and Trinity United Methodist Church. I am not sure when the cameras went up on the traffic lights downtown, but I only recently noticed them. They reflect an absence of neighborliness, and I resent their presence. Was there a debate about these, and I missed it? I often have my nose stuck in a dusty book of theology and, when driving, I spend more time with pop music than news radio. So I do miss things, and the cameras downtown came as an unpleasant surprise. I do not wish them well. This perspective may seem idiosyncratic. After all, aren't surveillance cameras the crucial key to solving grisly crimes on just about every BBC mystery? And, if I don't have anything to hide (except maybe my dorky dancing), and I stop obediently at every red light, why should I care if there are cameras up? I think in this case technology is a poor replacement for what we need

more of. That is, community. I'd rather have an over-abundance
of busybody, nosy neighbors watching one another's comings and
goings than cameras.

Conflicts about people and technology are key for plot lines
in much of North American literature, especially among novels set
in the future. I am teaching a class on sin in literature at a women's
prison in Raleigh, and we have been slogging through two different
dystopian, future worlds written by novelist Margaret Atwood. In
The Handmaid's Tale, the miserable future Atwood creates is held
together by a form of religious domination. Think Chairman Mao
plus John Calvin. In this fictional but creepily plausible scenario,
people are divided strictly into distinct roles, coerced through patterns of training to be isolated and alienated from one another, under the guise of unity. Key to the world of this particular novel is the
relative absence of technology. The form of religion used to control
the masses involves a forced turn backward. In lieu of computers,
for example, well-to-do women work on needlepoint and garden-
ing. (Not incidentally, women are also disallowed from reading.)
The surveillance that goes on in *The Handmaid's Tale* is principally
interpersonal, not technological. One of the warnings Atwood
gives is against nostalgia for the "good old days" when things were
supposedly simpler, before instant pudding and instant text mes-
saging. In her new dystopian trilogy, which begins with *Oryx and
Crake*, Atwood turns her critical sights on technology, describing a
society where people have become separated even from their own
bodies through the pervasive use of visual technologies. Under
perpetual scrutiny through surveillance, people in that imagined
future try to internalize the cameras, so to speak, watching others
on screen and filming themselves obsessively. In the process, they
become alienated from what most of us today would think of as
citizenship, neighborliness, or love.

I heard an interview on *The People's Pharmacy* recently that
helped me to articulate just why I care about those cameras downtown. The author of some new-fangled book or study or something
had "discovered" that surveillance cameras in medical settings
help keep doctors from making mistakes. If doctors know they are

being watched, in particular by other doctors, they are supposedly more careful with their patients. Or so the argument goes.

This just seemed nuts to me, as I listened, grumbled, and made breakfast, in part because I remember well hearing about another new-fangled study a while back that "discovered" that a great way to avoid medical error is to encourage actual people to watch out for one another. When orderlies, nurses, and doctors communicate with one another in the care of patients, fewer practitioners make mistakes. That study found that in settings where orderlies are encouraged to speak up when they see something awry, people fare better. And when nurses are encouraged to correct doctors when they notice a mistake, care improves. Basically, if people are encouraged to risk annoying one another and to speak up and out across the otherwise strict boundaries of authority in a hospital, it helps everyone do their job better. Of course, that sort of solution requires time-consuming practices to cultivate trust and patience, in an industry that is often more focused on the clock and the monetary bottom line. It is trickier to elicit genuine, abiding camaraderie than to put up cameras. Here, in our own beloved "City of Medicine," I would suggest we can do better than affix more confounded cameras around ourselves. Durhamites are capable of harder, and better, work than that.

P.S. There is a strand of political theology that defines the work of a public intellectual as advising people currently in power about how to wield their power responsibly. I disagree. I believe the work of a Christian theologian is best to define truth as one sees it, and to participate in the arduous, ongoing work of building open and transparent communication. I end this essay with a call for conversation about "better" rather than with a clear prescription for better. I hope to encourage people to talk to one another about what "better" looks like for our neighborhoods and schools. I am not interested in "casting a vision" as a leader. This is a moral conviction in itself—that sustained conversation about a polity, or about being a people, with real people, discussing our best judgements about living together, is the way God intended for us to be together at our best. As one student put it to me, a "visionary" in Christian terms is someone who sees visions of God's graced reality, and tells of those visions as part of a conversation. A "visionary" in business-speak (a language popular in some theological circles today) is someone who stands out in front of other people and tells them where they should be going. I aspire to be a visionary in Christian terms.

There are some essays in this collection where I have one very simple goal: to introduce the work of another writer so that people will look up their work and learn something new. In this essay, I quote a study by economist and social critic Dan Ariely. Dan Ariely was for some time a commentator on NPR, but, at least here in North Carolina, he has been replaced by someone whose analysis is much less politically radical than Ariely's. In this essay, I continue to try to encourage people to see the dignity of each child of God, while also recognizing the larger, social context of economic domination and dehumanization.

THE SHENANIGANS OF "RESPONSIBILITY" POLITICS

April, 2014

A media-savvy child of the new millennium, my older daughter is privy to all sorts of terms. This includes informally coined, succinct phrases to describe complicated concepts. These include phrases to label public conversations about tricky, politically charged issues. When I told her about the Moynihan Report from 1965, and gave her a thumbnail sketch, she rolled her eyes and groaned, "Responsibility politics." In case some readers are, like me, not clued in to this phrase, I will need to make a long story, well . . . long. Basically, the problematic idea my daughter named succinctly is the notion that social conditions for true human flourishing will come about by way of small, individually responsible changes. Reusable grocery bags are a helpful, simple example. There is something of a consensus that the environment matters. But, in many circles, the way environmentalism cashes out is through composting, recycling, and carrying around reusable grocery bags. Because bags are so public, they take on disproportional importance. If I am too darned tired after a long day to wash out yogurt containers and instead trash them, it is unlikely my neighbors will peek into my bin and call me out. Grocery bags are another matter. The polar bears are drowning, and you can't even be responsible for your grocery bags? Of course, that is silly. Plastic grocery bags are an infinitesimal part of the environmental problem. But, remembering my bags is a daily thing. The detrimental dumping practices of Duke Power is a giant, systemic thing. So, I walk around with my bags and my responsibility politics.

There is also a large dose of responsibility politics going on in the US regarding economic issues, during what many economists (and normal people) agree is the Second Great Depression. Maybe this is a kind of mental survival mechanism gone awry. If I think poverty and unemployment are primarily about individual responsibility, then maybe these problems will seem less humongous and insurmountable. Dan Ariely and Michael Norton found in a study they published in 2011 that most people in the US do not explicitly approve of the radical inequality we are swimming in right now, but we are in denial about how bad things really are. Again, maybe this is because most of us can't reckon with a giant mess. (Dan Ariely highlights on his website that our situation includes "the bottom 40% of Americans possessing less than 0.3% of total wealth" and "the top 20% possessing 84%.") Norton and Ariely found plenty of people who call themselves Republican as well as who call themselves Democrat who think the actual economic situation must surely be better than it is, and who, when asked about their ideal scenario, prefer an economic system that is even more equal than (gasp!) Sweden. Media conversations seem to eschew large, structural sorts of reasons for economic struggles. Stories reflect too often a form of responsibility politics, even when the story is ostensibly about a particular group. For example, a whole generation of college graduates has become a curiosity as, in story after story, we hear about those quirky young adults who, strangely enough, "choose" to live with their parents while working a hard-won, part-time job for minimum wage. Or, just recently, NPR played an ostensible human interest story about those plucky, middle-age professionals signing up for unpaid internships with the hope of new employment. And the middle-class success stories are often individual and morally soporific. Frankly, I think I will drown my radio if I hear one more perky feature about an inventive young teacher who, against all odds and drastic funding shortages, is quickening a love for Shakespeare in her overcrowded junior high classroom.

The tendency to individualize large problems suggests, in a more subtle way than the Moynihan Report did in 1965, that patterns of human diminishment and struggle are matters of individual or cohort pathology. If people in particular neighborhoods are drastically unemployed, then find a few heroes with moxie or discipline, recalibrate individual people's thinking, and life will be better for the 40 percent who possess 0.3 percent of the wealth. Or, if a generation of young adults can't find jobs, narrate desperation as the mother of ingenuity, and christen them as resiliently "creative." If people nearing retirement are being let go due to corporate downsizing, then maybe each one can find a computer screen and play those nifty memory enhancement games NPR just talked about until the economy recovers. I think the most insidious aspect of responsibility politics is that this way of thinking divides people from one another, allowing scarcity to seem ineluctable and casting our plight as a chance to distinguish ourselves as fit. I am holding out hope instead for abundance, and solidarity.

P.S. Many of the large pots of money for funding the field of "ethics" come from foundations or families who benefit greatly by an apolitical or even conservative form of "ethics." So, centers for ethics concentrate on how to encourage students not to cheat, not to post photos of themselves naked, and not actively to shout racist comments at one another. Duke is no different in this regard. There is a center for ethics here, and the conversations are often vaguely aesthetic and related to what my daughter named as "responsibility politics." Writing these essays has helped me to sort out how best to explain to Duke students why I am not so much interested in their recycling habits as I am their capacity to dig into the ways that power and money work in their own settings.

The preacher I quote below is Richard Hays. He was dean of Duke Divinity School and therefore my boss at the time I published this essay. I had to decide whether or not to name him here. Given that my essays had been consistently politically charged up to this point, I decided to leave his name out. I did write him a note before the essay appeared in print to let him know why I had not named him. He had told me in another conversation that he had been advised (I am not sure by whom) to be careful about his political statements as a Duke administrator. The core, theological affirmation of this essay is related to a book I was writing at the time, on a fourteenth-century visionary named Julian of Norwich.

EASTER TIDINGS

May, 2014

It is hard to talk about the resurrection of Jesus Christ without shame. The story is, at best, a strange story, and it has been used unabashedly to dominate non-Christians for centuries. But, before I go on, please note that this essay is not technically tardy. For Christians, Eastertide begins on Easter Sunday and lasts fifty days. Taylor Mills, the pastor at Trinity United Methodist, has told the congregation twice recently that Eastertide is ten days longer than Lent. If I knew that fact before this Easter, I had forgotten it. There is a historical explanation for the particular length of Lent and Eastertide, but I am going to make up a reason to fit my argument. Some Christians find Easter even less believable than Lent. It takes us ten extra days past Lent to practice actual joy in Eastertide.

A preacher I knew many moons ago at Yale gave a sermon contrasting responses to Easter by imagining two early followers of Jesus: Doubting Thomas and his twin, "Believin'" Stephen. Stephen didn't need to see Jesus in the flesh, much less see Jesus' wounds. Stephen went around winning people by proclaiming "Jesus is Lord!" Thomas needed to see Jesus in the flesh and to see the actual wounds of the cross on Jesus. Even non-Christians may have heard the term "Doubting Thomas," because his story of skepticism hits a nerve. Thomas suspected that the words he was hearing about the resurrection of Jesus were the collectively delusional wishes of Jesus' disciples. Or, maybe Thomas thought the disciples had been bought off by the authorities to postpone a revolution. In saying they'd seen Jesus alive, maybe they were placating the decadently evil Roman Empire. Or, maybe the resurrection story of Jesus Christ was wishful thinking *and* political spin, the worst of both worlds (pious and political).

The passage in the Gospel of John, a passage that has come now to be popularly known as the story of Doubting Thomas, is the Gospel reading that every United Methodist minister is supposed to read each Sunday after Easter, year after year. If a United Methodist preacher preaches about the resurrection on the second Sunday of Eastertide, she can't easily avoid the question posed by Doubting Thomas. Is the resurrection story truth, or delusion, or spin, or some convoluted combination of all three?

The contrast in the sermon on Believin' Stephen and Doubting Thomas depends on a difference between a false joy of denial and a joy that endures right in the turmoil of reality. Thomas may have insisted on seeing the wounds of the cross on the body of Jesus Christ because he could not believe in a Lord and Savior that did not bear the signs of the cross. As Gillian Welch sings in "By the Mark," these signs are how "the King of Heaven can be told from the prince of fools." This way of reading the story has implications for real, live churches, in that churches are to be the "body of Christ" in the world. If a congregation professes a faith that bears no marks of the evil around us and between us, then that congregation is an impostor. The gift is to receive faith right alongside the bloody truth.

There is a form of Christian joy open to derision right now. These churches fall under the descriptive term "Prosperity Gospel." My colleague, Kate Bowler, has written a fabulous book on this movement, and Barbara Ehrenreich helpfully locates the trend more broadly in *Bright-Sided*. But I am concerned with another tendency in American Christianity, a heresy that I will call the "Austerity Gospel." In this form of the Gospel of Jesus Christ, the way to winning God's approval is to accept your own suffering as part of winning. If the "Prosperity Gospel" of Easy Easter and Believin' Stephen is about praying yourself to a big winning lottery ticket, then the Austerity Gospel is about making yourself as insignificant as possible, and as guilty as possible, in order to win favor from God. In this false mode of faith, I hope to find some success or mere safety within the brutality of the world by rendering myself abject and compliant. The key terms in churches that are part of the Gospel of Austerity are *obedience*, the word *just* (as in, I "just" can't begin to deserve anything), and *Lordship*. I don't think the Gospel of Austerity is the true alternative to Easy Easter. The resurrected body of Jesus bears the wounds of evil in the world, and yet is tenaciously tilted toward true joy. Jesus is not a body made of titanium. It is a body that still bears the wounds, and yet still dances toward heaven.

P.S. This is a theme that is central to my teaching, shaped in part by my many students who have been caught up in one gimmick or another to justify their existence on this earth. The next essay follows simply on this one, and has at the core this same central theme. But it raised a ruckus.

PORNOGRAPHY

June, 2014

I am a Christian ethicist, and I teach about sex. So, I've had way, way too many former students send me emails about the student at Duke who has helped pay her college tuition by performing sexual relations with men while being filmed. My gut reaction to the news story was simple. If she performs one act of heterosexual sex on film once a month she is making $10,000 more than I am after teaching for fifteen years at Duke.

But I am at heart (if not gut) a Methodist minister, so my next thought was "What Would Jesus Do?" Jesus would ask the "Duke Porn Star" if he could have dinner at her dorm with her friends and then wash everyone's feet. Jesus would not have been sexy with the young woman trying to make her way through college by being a part of the pornography industry. Jesus would have ignored the sex trade industry and instead tried to be her actual friend. This complicated reply to former students who'd sent me irate emails confused them, or made them angry. Here I will try to confuse readers by comparing pornography to online learning. And, as if that is not confusing enough, I will also compare churches that use video screens to XXX cinemas.

In the argot of pornography, a key word is *perform*. What does it mean to "perform" a sexual activity with another person? It means to be an actor, not oneself. To "perform" means to follow a script, to be a character different than oneself, and to disconnect from the reactive parts of your soul. The person watching another person on film "performing" a sexual act is not engaging with a person. That person is reacting to a human trying to "perform." The last time so many students sent me a link to read about pornography was when John Mayer had an interview with *Playboy* confessing (among even more miserable things) to having viewed

300 photos of women's private parts before crawling out of bed some mornings. What made me sad then and still makes me sad now is that this man felt safer with photographs and films of parts of women than with a real woman herself. I wish for him the courage to wake up each morning with the same, real person and know himself beloved.

Now to "MOOCs" or Massive Open Online Courses—a big fad right now. A student I taught a decade ago said that the problem with academics is that we all had to beg for a date to the prom. Many academics are insecure, whether because we were too smart or too hairy or too tall or too short, and we are susceptible to the allure of being accepted. So, if you tell one of us that we would be really good at giving a TED sort of talk (on video, with a snappy theme) then we might feel like we have been finally invited to the prom by a popular kid. We might then be more likely to agree in general to more MOOCs and fewer actual classrooms with real people. But, to "do" a TED talk, or to "teach" a MOOC is a performance. Good teaching requires a kind of trust and openness to new ideas and new voices that real intimacy also entails. At my best, as a teacher, I try to hear, and sort out, and reconsider, and hear again, and remain open. Granted, teaching this way sometimes makes me nearly sick with fear, but I re-enter the pedagogical fray and facilitate the eyeball-to-eyeball, soul-to-soul conversations that happen at the intersection of truth.

The place where I have been taught to trust actual people is an actual church. I grew up a preacher's daughter in West Texas, and I don't idealize the mess that is "church." Churches are made of people, after all. Similar to MOOCs, a new trend for super-churches is to use video technology to broadcast the leading leader, sometimes across states, in different church buildings. I submit to such leaders that it is better to trust another person to be in the pulpit, not performing but actually preaching, than to ask someone to pull down a video screen and introduce your disembodied self to a room full of people. My father has an apropos rule for this. He told an aspiring pastor that he should not appear on a televised screen for a "satellite campus" on Sunday mornings because parishioners "need to be able to smell you."

So, for the sake of actual love, and actual teaching, and actual preaching, I suggest that the real problem with pornography is *performance*. Sex, love, teaching, and preaching should be about real people—smelly, scary, and beautiful.

P.S. My younger daughter overheard a conversation about this essay. When I explained a bit of the backstory, her first response was that she hopes the young woman who was at the center of the controversy has read my words, and that she feels better about the fact that not everyone is judging her. My daughter's very mature perspective was not shared by everyone. I often receive emails or letters about my writing. This essay prompted one Methodist layman to write a long missive to several bishops, the dean of Duke Divinity School, the president of Duke University, and dozens of other people. As with all mail that is vaguely threatening, I glanced over the note to see if he had included anything like "I know where you live." He had not, so I hit delete. But one of the people included in his message took his words very seriously. I ended up in a senior administrator's office having a very strange conversation about whether or not I had been sufficiently clear that Jesus would have condemned pornography. This was one of those totally bizarre intersections of church and academy. The most clearly controversial aspect of this essay is that I was stating publicly that I am against online classes—a trend that had been touted that very month on the cover of the Duke alumni magazine. But, instead of discussing the importance of in-person pedagogy, I ended up having to explain to someone who should have known better that, while Jesus told a woman to "Go, and sin no more," he did not walk up to her and use those words to put her in an obedient trance, like a magician. Jesus did not work that way, thank God. So, I stand by this piece. I do not believe it is "disgraceful," as the senior administrator asserted. I suggest it is testimony to grace.

After that aforementioned, unpleasant, meeting about pornography, I went to report the conversation to the appropriate office at Duke. I struck up a conversation in the waiting room, with a women who happened also to be there. When people ask me what I do for a living, I usually explain that I am a teacher, but sometimes we end up talking about my work as a writer as well. In this case, I explained that I write a monthly column for the paper. This new friend, a friend in a waiting room, gave me permission to write about forgiveness in a way that begins with her words. It was one of those snippets of life that, as a Christian, I considered a miracle. Her trust in me allowed me to write something that ended up being helpful to other women and men who needed to hear this word.

UNRECONCILED

July, 2014

"I know I have to forgive him, because otherwise I won't get into heaven." A friend said this to me recently about someone who had treated her horribly. Casting forgiveness as a duty is one take-away message from the New Testament. But how did that particular bumper sticker receive such tenaciously sticky backing in evangelical circles? Harboring a spirit of revenge is exhausting, even toxic. But carrying around the burden to forgive can also warp a soul. A song I sang as a kid goes: "So high, you can't get over it. So low, you can't get under it. So wide, you can't get around it. You gotta go in through the door." I remember being told that door was Jesus Christ. How did my own will to forgive become the door to heaven?

A few years ago David Crabtree interviewed me about John Edwards. My answers reflect my crushed hopes that John and Elizabeth Edwards were going to facilitate change in the South. I answered David's question about forgiveness from the gut, and accidentally got it right. The idea that anyone in the Edwards family had a responsibility to forgive John Edwards seemed off. I had heard people in evangelical circles ask a similar question about the Mark Sanford and John Ensign debacles. Don't family members have a *responsibility* to reconcile? When asked about one of my own fallen heroes, I said something controversial, but consistent. No.

I believe no one wronged by another human being has a responsibility to reconcile, for two reasons. First, forgiveness is God's work. To ask a mere mortal to make forgiveness their duty is to mistake a person for Jesus. Second, I have heard the term "reconciliation" used to elide the ramifications of injustice. The word is often used more for opacity than truth. Camera operators apply a thin layer of petroleum jelly to the lens before an actor's close-up—to make the image more "forgiving." "Reconciliation" has been used like petroleum jelly in some circles—to blur the truth. Spokesmen have told people who have suffered injustice to focus their spiritual energy right back onto their former relationship to an individual or a group that has wronged them, and then used the blurring power of "reconciliation" to smooth over the fractures of that wrong.

This constitutes religious gas-lighting. In case that term is unfamiliar, here is a definition from Wikipedia: "Gaslighting or gas-lighting is a form of mental abuse in which false information is presented with the intent of making victims doubt their own memory, perception, and sanity." Take, for example, a commonly used biblical passage from 2 Corinthians: "And all things are of God, who hath reconciled us to himself by Jesus Christ, and hath given to us the ministry of reconciliation." Whatever this means to a Christian surviving or recovering from injustice, such passages should not be used to conjure an alternative world where wounds are healed because a third party has described them as healed. I have seen "reconciliation" used like a Jedi mind trick. A Christian leader with sufficient training can almost convince a human being that she didn't see what she saw and did not suffer what she knows she suffered.

A Christian leader whose name became synonymous with "reconciliation" is Desmond Tutu, for his work with the Truth and Reconciliation Commission in South Africa. His name has come up again recently, with an emphasis on "truth" and the invasion of Iraq. In July, 2012, at a forum on faith and public life, Tony Blair again denied praying with George W. Bush about invading Iraq. Several weeks after the event, Archbishop Tutu publicly refused to appear at a conference on "eadership" with Tony Blair. "If leaders may lie, then who should tell the truth?" Tutu asks in his September 1, 2012 essay for *The Observer*. Tutu suggests Bush and Blair "should be made to answer for their actions in The Hague," and reminds readers: "Good leaders are the custodians of morality."

I want in closing to ask about the glue that has made a bumper sticker version of forgiveness so tenaciously sticky. The Fellowship Foundation facilitates the colossal, week-long spectacle of faith and leadership that is the National Prayer Breakfast. The word *reconciliation* appears repeatedly on their official website, and I heard "reconciliation" used as often as "Jesus" when I attended the Prayer Breakfast two years ago. I think the concept is being used to dupe perpetrators as well as survivors, encouraging obliviousness or cynicism. (Blair and Bush have displayed both.) Reading Tutu's words, and thinking about what truthful reconciliation must mean—whether in matters of war, or domestic violence, or racism, or geopolitics—another "R" word comes to mind. That word is "reparations." I'd like some glue on that bumper sticker.

P.S. I am very grateful to David Crabtree for interviewing me and also for telling me that my words on forgiveness could be pastorally helpful to others. I am also grateful to friends in London who pointed out the story about Desmond Tutu and Tony Blair. The coverage of that story in the US was sparse, at best, but accountability for the war in Iraq continues to be a matter of Christian ethics in some circles.

I started this essay with a memory that I could not confirm. That is, I remembered country western star Barbara Mandrell singing the "union label" song when I was a child. But then I could not for the life of me receive confirmation that my memory was correct. I had to rewrite the first paragraph three times trying to fact-check my very young memories from the 1970s. I did receive confirmation from an archivist at Cornell that the Mandrell Sisters actually sang the "union label" song on their television show! I am very grateful to Patrizia Sione, research archivist at the Kheel Center for Labor Management Documentation & Archives at Cornell, who wrote me this note a few weeks after this essay ran: "The Union Label Song was sung on the Mandrell Sisters Show in the 1970s (from the General Executive Board Report to the 38th Convention, International Ladies Garment Workers' Union, 1983, page 74)." Thank God for archivists! Without a detailed, nuanced account of history, it is hard to diagnose the present. This piece was also inspired by the work of the "Backstory Radio" podcasts, which I recommend heartily for anyone trying to say anything truthful about political theology in the US today.

THE UNION LABEL

August, 2014

When I was a child, a catchy advertisement aired between reruns of *Scooby Doo* and *Josie and the Pussy Cats*. It went like this: "Look for the union label/When you are buying a coat, dress, or blouse/ Remember somewhere our union's sewing/Our wages going to feed the kids and run the house!" The one that aired in Texas was introduced by an avuncular, southern man wearing a bolo tie. I thus have early associations of unions and the country music show *Hee Haw*. Like the "Made in the USA" ads from 1986 (featuring Bob Hope and Carol Channing) the "union label" advertisements encouraged work with dignity in the textile industry. My mom was a teacher, and my cousins were actors, so I heard stories from them about how unions also helped women to educate or entertain without exploitation. Labor unions seemed to me as American as apple pie.

My first summer home from college I worked at a law office. I thought I might go into law, and the job paid slightly more than babysitting. I was as inquisitive then as now, so I read things as I made copies. I figured out pretty quickly that two senior partners were defending big oil companies against people who had been injured or killed on the job, or loved ones left behind. The firm that filed workers' compensation suits was in a building even fancier than ours, so I was disabused early of the idea that I could just switch sides and be made righteous. I knew kids whose fathers worked in oil fields. They were not raking in the financial benefits of a system that exploited people on the job. But the heads of both law firms had homes with swimming pools, and not the kind you use an air pump to inflate. Maybe juries made up of people in states with anti-labor laws are more prone to award large sums to someone who has been egregiously wronged at work. I reckoned that a brutal way to win in a broken system. Also, the rules by which a normal person could gain a settlement or win a suit seemed as reckless and random as a state-run lottery. It was a precipitous decision, but I decided then against law school.

I chose instead the inviolable institution that is "the academy." (That was irony.) While going to graduate school in one of the most union-infused states, I not only learned four languages but also the inflection of life at an organization patterned by labor unions. Professors were not unionized, but they benefited from the fact that people who worked in the support services were. At both the Divinity School and in the Religious Studies Department, people took time actually to eat lunch away from their desks. Many professors went home around 5, because a 9 to 5 rhythm was a norm established through arduous, union organizing for decades by the women (and most of them were women) who did the work with paper and numbers and copiers and such, work that allows scholars to do the differently hard tasks of teaching and writing pristine prose. I was privy to the benefits of a university that actually did take time to sleep. I trained for the Christian ministry and, eventually, for the theological academy, at a place that held the wisdom of Sabbath rest more seriously than many churches I know.

In my dream Oscar speech, I'd have lots of people to thank for being able to complete my PhD at a swanky school, but I would have to include my friends with whom I organized for the graduate student labor union. "Our work makes Yale work" was our motto, and we shared it with members of the two established unions there. Sitting in strategy meetings with electricians and clerical workers, historians and anthropologists, I learned a way of thinking about my work that is best characterized by the word "solidarity." The academy can be as unapologetically competitive as a cage fight. And an elite university can be every bit as arbitrary in meting out reward and punishment as the workers' compensation game in Texas. But in organizing I learned how to compete with my own best self, not over and against my peers. Along with the people baking bread or painting dorm room walls, we took pride in our labor, and I learned what it feels like to work with dignity. Today, if someone asks me the scriptural basis for the pro-union label, this is my best answer. Labor unions are a tried and true way to remind yourself, your co-workers, and your boss that you are a human being, worthy of respect. You are not a tool. I think God approves of that.

There is a radio show that runs on my local National Public Radio station called "Fresh Air." The host of the show, Terry Gross, tried to interview Gene Simmons, of Kiss fame, for her show. It was a disaster, by all accounts, but hilariously so. I cannot recommend you listen to it, because Simmons has not given permission for the show to run audio or a transcript of the interview. But I heard it when it originally aired, and I remember well that Simmons gave a brilliant account of why the band wore make-up. He explained that men wore make-up for the same reason that women sometimes wear make-up: for courage. He talked about how putting on a face can help you be courageous. I think of that often when I am visiting my favorite make-up counter. But, in this essay, I still hold Gene Simmons responsible for being icky.

A GRACIOUS RESPONSE TO CHIVALRY

September, 2014

My daughters had an exchange about tween boys two years ago. My younger daughter was complaining about her fifth grade class. My older daughter asked: "Are the boys still making [flatulence] noises with their armpits?" Apparently they were. "Well," she reassured her sister, "they will stop that soon, and then school isn't so bad."

Back in my own fifth grade days, when dinosaurs roamed the earth, I endured flatulence jokes, but also something more annoying. Too many fifth grade boys I knew, or barely knew, were sticking their tongues out as far as they could when girls walked by. I was baffled. Why were boys walking around sticking out their tongues? My mother, a public school teacher, explained that for some boys even negative attention felt better than no attention. She told me to ignore them, and they would stop. That made sense, sort of. But I was still confused they were not simply tripping me or pulling my hair like they used to. Then I saw the cover of an album by the bubblegum rock group Kiss. It was right there. Clear as day.

Gene Simmons, the lead "singer" of the band, was teaching boys they could get attention from girls by sticking out their tongues. I hold a grudge against Gene Simmons to this day. My dream team of people who will be stranded together in purgatory with Donald Rumsfeld and Margaret Thatcher always includes Gene Simmons. So, although I initially had a different focus in mind for this month's essay, I have to respond to Gene's televised defense of chivalry. One of television's many pseudo-news channels has a show during which beautiful women sit around talking about things that women are told to care about, and Gene was brought on to talk about the importance of chivalry. Among other silly things he said, Gene exclaimed that he wishes women still wanted to have our doors opened for us. As Amanda Marcotte explained in her article for *Slate*, "the woman who angrily dresses down a man for daring to open the door for her is the Bigfoot of feminism." OK, here you have to be patient with me and Amanda Marcotte. The first time I heard "Bigfoot of feminism" I was also confused. So, let me explain the phrase in plain terms. Bigfoot is a pretend creature meant to scare and attract attention. Women who don't want doors held open for them are pretend, because people generally like to have doors held open for them. So, the story that there are feminists out there who are disgusted when a man opens the door for them is a story that is made up to scare people. Gene Simmons went on a rant on television about women who do not exist. So, now, to connect the dots, Gene Simmons, who encouraged adolescent boys of my generation to be gross, has gone on a pseudo-news channel to defend chivalry and to encourage hate about feminism. The irony is so deep I don't know whether to laugh or pray.

Here is what I do know. Where I grew up, holding the door open for anyone was basic. It might mean you cost an establishment extra money on air conditioning, but you hold the door open for the next person. I also learned from my parents that love after war or during a recession required everyone to drop the facade of chivalry and practice human decency. Male or female, we need one another to open doors and change diapers and wash dishes. And, if a man comes home from war unable to carry his beloved over the threshold, that does not make him less of a man. And, if a woman comes home from war too distracted by the trauma of combat to bake a cherry pie, then, well . . . Billy Boy had better learn to bake a cherry pie, and to share it with his family. (That is a reference to a song from when my grandparents were young.)

My older daughter shared a photo with me last year that takes this message deeper than my own father ever intended. It has a photo of a man wearing a T-shirt with a list: "Rules for dating my daughter. I don't make the rules. You don't make the rules. She makes the rules. Her body, her rules." It would represent a giant leap for good manners if each girl child were taught to know what is and is not attractive to her. (Displaying your tongue is as gross as armpit jokes. And defending chivalry is repulsive.) And, dear daughters of mine, it is not a betrayal of good manners to know your own body, and to make your own good rules.

P.S. It says something about the setting in which I often teach that it felt courageous to type up that last paragraph. Writing as a feminist in an evangelical institution has not been simple. But this essay helped me build toward a later essay on girl power. When I look back at these monthly offerings, I am struck by how they are sometimes like bread crumbs I was leaving for myself, guiding my way toward writing more courageously, with or without lipstick.

I wanted to write an essay about gentrification in Durham, but I was not sure where to start, and how to reach a wider audience than the usual suspects. This little groundhog showed up, in the midst of something very serious taking place in my neighborhood. As I type this introduction, the shed in which the groundhog hid is being replaced by a new building. While many people talk about Durham's progress, that "progress" is white and upper class.

A GROUNDHOG TALE FROM GREEN STREET

October, 2014

There are two shops on Ninth Street in Durham featuring different messages about our dear city. One has a T-shirt in the window that says "Durham, It's Not For Everyone." Another features a T-shirt that says "Durham, It's For Everyone." I love both stores, but I like the second T-shirt better. I want Durham to be for everyone, and I have my own "honey-do list" for the city's leaders. (My magic wand is broken, so I make lists.) First on the list is my wish that the fabulous "Bull City Connector" bus would actually connect *both* historic universities in Durham to downtown and to one another. But that is for another post.

Something happened in my neighborhood last week that brought home again how Durham is still not "for everyone." Two elderly neighbors were given mere weeks to move out of the duplex they'd lived in for years, and a displaced groundhog ended up standing her ground in my alley. In the process, I have learned something about wildlife in the city. I was also struck again by how swiftly a neighborhood can be moved around like children's building blocks. Only, actual people live in these blocks.

When I bought my house on Green Street fourteen years ago, a friend warned I was going to be part of the gentrification of the neighborhood. He was right. Brought up on Sesame Street, I wanted to live in a diverse neighborhood where people know one another, the name of the person carrying the mail, and the people

53

at Mr. Hooper's store. (That's for old school Sesame Street fans.) Several years after my family moved in, families living in apartments in the house next door were told to move out, because the owner of the building was going to renovate and sell. The house sat vacant for two years, then was refurbished and sold. Neighbors told me to be glad, because the process had increased my property value. I wasn't so sure that this is what progress in Durham looks like, for me or for my neighbors. I like my new neighbors, but I also liked my old neighbors. It was around that time that I heard a term applicable to Durham: "doughnut city." The term gives a visual image of what is happening in many cool cities in the US. People who can afford to approximate Sesame Street live in the middle, and people who can't afford to stay are pushed to the outer circle. David Byrne has a great quote that goes, "Rich people will travel great distances to look at poor people." A variation would be that some rich people like me will pay lots of money to live next to poor people, only the poor people then have to move.

One of my neighbors who had to move last week had a tiny dog that looked like the muppet Fizzgig from the movie *The Dark Crystal*. When allowed outside, this Fizzgig would yap ferociously, right next to a warning sign featuring a barking Doberman. (There was no Doberman.) When the owners of the duplex decided to have the entire thicket next to the duplex razed, it became clear why Fizzgig had been barking. There were families of rabbits and birds and at least one groundhog living there. The story that went through my head as the animals wandered around disoriented in the streets and yards around the gaping hole that was their home is *Mrs. Frisby and the Rats of NIMH*, by Robert C. O'Brien. O'Brien won a Newberry for the book in 1972, and it is an intricate story of neighbors, resistance, and community organizing. I have no medically enhanced, genius rats in my neighborhood, so I called the Museum of Life and Science, the Ellerbe Creek Watershed Association and, eventually CLAWS, Inc., who proved to be our heroes. (Look them up at www.nc-claws.org.) George, from CLAWS, came to my house and explained to me that a groundhog and a woodchuck are the same animal, and that I should leave the groundhog to establish her new home in a nearby shed. Evidently, for all their cuteness, groundhogs are really fierce. I now imagine the Green Street groundhog has made friends with Mrs. Frisby, and, with the rats displaced by the nearby hotel, they are plotting for a new thicket.

Here is another wish, less fanciful but still tricky. I wish that even more of the same people who love Ellerbe Creek and the Beaver Queen Pageant and CLAWS would join with community groups resisting evictions, rent rate hikes, and the doughnut-ification of Durham in neighborhoods like Old North Durham (to name one example). I wish for Durham more crisscrossing, plotting alliances to make Durham a place truly for everyone.

P.S. I should have been more direct in this essay. I was implicitly tying together two different conversations in Durham. The Ellerbe Creek Watershed Association holds a fantastic festival every year called the Beaver Queen Pageant. It is a fundraiser for the Watershed Association, and it features many ribald, joyful references to women's sexuality. I attended for the first time right after my divorce, and I blushed repeatedly. I was inspired, though, by the ways that women who are older than I am can celebrate their beautiful bodies with no ounce of shame. There are many wonderful women who have brought this pageant together each year, but I wish more of them would use their creativity to protest the ways that our city has become inhospitable to human animals. I love my neighborhood, but, judging by the items on the email LISTSERV, we are often more concerned to protect songbirds by putting bells on cats than we are about how our neighborhood is becoming whiter and wealthier with each passing year.

I do not experience "community" on social media, but I do find online media helpful at times. For instance, in this case, one little "tweet" (meaning a very short message) on the social networking site Twitter seemed helpful to many ministers who were trying to figure out how to preach in the warlock's brew of fear-mongering that went on right before the midterm elections in 2014. I am grateful for the many people who "retweeted" this message on their own forms of social media. But, more importantly, I am grateful to the fourteenth-century visionary who risked heresy to write hopefully rather than submissively.

LAUGH AT THE DEVIL

November, 2014

I've learned how to "tweet." This involves putting words together to share, using 140 characters. One of my most "retweeted" "tweets" on the Internet came out after a tragedy had everyone in panic mode. These were the words: "The world is transfixed by fear. Perfect love whispers in fear's ear to turn his head toward hope."

I was paraphrasing a fourteenth-century mystic, Julian of Norwich. I am writing a book about what her visions have taught me about fear. She is really in my head this week because, according to every news media outlet around us, we are supposed to be scared of one another. Restaurants, waiting rooms, and the pump at my gas station have news blaring: EBOLA! ISIS! Short of sleeping at the Eno River, you too will be exposed to the contagion of FEAR.

I recommend an antidote. But first, a history lesson. Julian of Norwich is the name given to the woman who wrote the first book written in English attributed to a woman. We don't know what name "Julian of Norwich" answered to before she came to be called "Julian of Norwich." We refer to her by that because, toward the end of her life, she was a resident wise woman in a church in Norwich, England that had long been called St. Julian's. Sometime near the late fourteenth century, this woman took the name of St.

Julian's church in Norwich. The church was bombed to oblivion by the German air force during World War II. But it was rebuilt for people who have the means to travel and love the writer known as Julian of Norwich. Tourists who don't know a fig about the second-century St. Julian go there because they think Mother Julian, from the fourteenth century, was holy. They go to see the apartment she lived in, adjacent to the place where people received Mass (the Lord's Supper or Holy Communion) and feel close to her.

Norwich, England was a port city. In the fourteenth century there were "sumptuary laws" in England. This meant that peasants, farmers, and other human beings without certifiably blue blood were forbidden to dress in a way that might allow them to pass above their station. As a port, Norwich had people coming in ships from Europe, dressed in ways that could not be easily sorted. Also, the official English church at this time distributed the Lord's Supper, or Communion, according to rank and station. The first were to be first to the table, and the middle to be middle, and the last to be very, very last. If there was no more bread by then, so be it. Christianity, as it was practiced in the beautiful, fancy churches that people pay good money to see, was practiced during Julian of Norwich's time to remind everyone to keep in their place. And, well . . . then there was the plague. Thousands of people during this period were dying, horribly and suddenly. And they were dying "unshriven." There were so few priests left alive in some areas to deliver the last rites to the dying that people were dying without being cared for to say confession and receive blessing. People left behind were stricken with fear that their husband, mother, or child was condemned to hell.

Norwich also had what came to be known as "Lollard's Pit," a place where heretics were brought by the church authorities to be burned alive. Fourteenth-century followers of a man named John Wycliffe, a group known pejoratively as "the Lollards," were thrown in a pit and burned alive as examples of how *not* to think around the time that Julian of Norwich was bravely trying to write down what she had seen. The Lollards were in trouble for suggesting that regular people ought to be able to read the Bible. This was a dangerous suggestion. If regular people started reading the Bible themselves, they might believe they could think for themselves, without the strictly hierarchical authority of the feudal and church systems. Wycliffe and his band of merry men and women had caught an idea that was irrepressible throughout early Christian history. No matter the chaos and rules around you, Jesus had given a new rule. Sit down and eat with your brothers and sisters. And, by the way, your brothers and sisters are those you most fear.

When Julian of Norwich wrote, people were dying by the thousands of disease. People were scared of newcomers, given that they could be carriers of disease, chaos, or heresy. And, Christians were being hanged for saying that Jesus did not care much for the stupid rank and file system. Her answer? Laugh at the devil. Look to Jesus. Keep hope. And don't let fear be your new religion.

P.S. I am very grateful to a friend who works in medieval history who helped me to understand how better to describe the disparate movement that I collapsed under the too-simple heading of "Lollards" in this essay. I drew heavily on this essay for a public talk I gave on public health at Emory University a few weeks later and another one at Princeton Seminary several months later. Writing 800 words on a writer as complicated as Julian of Norwich helped me to create a sort of literary chicken stock. I concentrated down what I thought was most important in her writing, for readers in the US today, and I then used that chicken stock repeatedly as I lectured and, eventually, completed a small book on her writings. The title of that book is *Laughing at the Devil*.

As I wrote before, I sometimes write an essay around an anchoring prayer that someone who reads the essay will look up a name that might be otherwise lost in the maelstrom of pop culture. My father loves Tom Lehrer. It was an aspect of my father's personality that sometimes confused me as a child. I would see glimmers of my father's sense of irony in his sermons, but Tom Lehrer was so unabashedly political and ironic. I almost converted to Judaism when I was a first-year student at Emory, in no small part because none of the Jewish men I met at Emory said anything even remotely like "be grateful" or "God's will" or other platitudes of meaningless obedience that I was hearing from some Christian men in my life. I am grateful that gratitude comes as a gift to me often, and daily. I have been able somehow to hear God's gift of gratitude almost every day of my almost-half-century life. But to be told to be grateful is not helpful, at least not in my experience. So, here is my offering on gifts, which I wrote right as I was about to host my family for Christmas in 2014.

MY FAVORITE THINGS

December, 2014

For my twelfth birthday my dad took a group of my friends and I to the local theater. I can't remember what movie we saw, but I do remember that night. I was small for my age and planning to take advantage of the child's ticket price well into my teens. But my father corrected me, in front of the manager. I had to pay the adult price from then on. And, from then on, we called my father "Honest Abe." My father is painfully honest. Even when he wants to tell a little lie, as in response to "Dad, does this dress look good?" he can't. He tries, but it is written all over his face. As a minister, who has to sit up front during a poorly performed choir anthem, this trait has not served him well. My family can tell our favorite stories about his grimaces. My dad cannot feign appreciation.

I have a godson who has become notorious for his painful honesty. He cannot pretend to like a gift, even if it was carefully handmade by his grandmother. This has caused no end of embarrassment, but I think the apple has fallen close to the "Honest Abe" tree. He does not like to be toyed with. It took him years to accept my joke that I was not just his godmother but his "fairy godmother." "There's no such thing!" When he first heard a description of the Lord's Supper as Jesus' body and Jesus' blood, he was disgusted, and declared he was not going to be participating in that ritual anymore. No amount of spiritualizing helped, because, each week, he'd be reminded of the actual words said. Either the priest up there talking at the table is lying, or not. This child could not feign appreciation for a gift he thought was gross.

The season between Thanksgiving and Christmas is a time when we are told, repetitively, to be grateful. The comedian Tom Lehrer wrote a song released in 1965 about the silliness of pretending to be grateful for one another when we are not actually grateful at all. The song is called "National Brotherhood Week," and you can find it on the Internet. The sentiment of the actual National Brotherhood Week—originally a week of religious toleration in dreary February—may have been beautifully truthful. But in his introduction to the televised debut of his song, Lehrer said these words:

> During National Brotherhood Week various special events are arranged to drive home the message of brotherhood. This year, for example, on the first day of the week, Malcolm X was killed, which gives you an idea of how effective the whole thing is. I'm sure we all agree that we ought to love one another, and I know there are people in the world who do not love their fellow human beings, and I hate people like that!

My father had a cassette tape of Tom Lehrer songs that we played in the car on our long way to visit extended family at Thanksgiving. I learned to sing along with gusto to "National Brotherhood Week." Being unable to feign appreciation for artifice can be a complicated gift. Tom Lehrer, my father, and my godson are each speakers of inconvenient truths.

I am now going to say something offensive: gratitude is not a virtue. Gratitude is not a habit of the heart that you can practice. You can practice pretense. You can practice a pretty smile or a vague, avuncular gaze. But you cannot make yourself grateful. Gratitude is a gift. Gratitude comes as a surprise, often when you are going about your normal day, sometimes when you are grouchy. That was the way of the shepherds, watching their flocks by night. And it is the way of the miracles I have received in Durham during my fifteen years here. I am grateful for Mariya Tivnan, who I met on Ninth Street over a decade ago and who has given me not only pretty highlights and haircuts but also insight. I am grateful for David McKnight, who I also met on Ninth Street, who sings the best version of "Amy" I have ever heard and is a teller of many truths. I am grateful for the members of the Trinitarian Class at Trinity UMC. I am grateful for the people who work at Kroger on North Pointe who have helped me find and then check out items a thousand times. These are a few of my favorite things.

There are truths that need to be told about the history and present of Durham. Pretending we all get along or that we can easily learn to get along is insipid. I trust the miracles of unexpected friendships and stories truthfully told will continue, God willing.

P.S. Many people told me this essay was wrongheaded. Many people believe that gratitude can be cultivated. I continue to believe and to experience that gratitude is a surprising gift.

Even while I wrote this essay, I suspected that the Durham police were being fitted with cameras on their helmets. While on social media, I had seen post after post after post calling for police officers to have cameras affixed to their helmets, by online "activists" and then repeated by friends who take much of what they see posted by online "activists" to be truth. I did not expect to stem this tide. But I wanted at least to register that I thought it was deeply wrong, and divisive, to turn more police officers into machines. They are not machines. They are human beings.

ON THE ELEVENTH DAY OF CHRISTMAS

January, 2015

I have written posts for the *Durham Herald-Sun* against surveillance cameras, online classes, virtual sex, and preaching by remote. Putting cameras on police helmets is also a bad idea. Durham should not be a city of alienated strangers. There are many arguments against turning people into automated enforcers of order. This is a Christian one.

While I write this column, my church is celebrating the twelve days between Christmas Day and Epiphany. Christmas is about learning one more time how to love your family even while weary or hyped up on sugar. It is also about being patient with people you have never met while waiting in line at Kroger. It is about lights and candles and eggnog and those cute little ham biscuits and football. But, for Christians, at the center of all the busyness and kitsch is the birth of a baby who we believe is God-with-us. Christians believe God became flesh and dwelt among us. In other words, we believe that God so loved the world God became a person, like us, because that was the best way God could know and love us. This is really basic. There may be some years the incarnation seems impossible. There may be years when baking cookies covers the pain of winter despair. There may be years when you and God are not on speaking terms and you attend services out of habit. But there is no getting around the fact that Christians are supposed to celebrate a little baby made of both God stuff and human stuff, all mixed together to save the world.

After Christians celebrate the Christian New Year during Advent, the belief that God became human spirals outward to light up other practices. When Christians repeat a reading from the Gospel of Matthew that says "where two or three are gathered," we don't mean gathered online. I have heard arguments for and against friendships on the Internet, but the incarnation stipulates that "gathered" means actually being face-to-face, hearing one another voice to ear—being in one another's real presence. Granted, being in the same space together is not sufficient to guarantee you actually recognize that there is another human being beside you. You can ignore that the being in front of you is human. But being actually present is necessary for what Christians call "fellowship." To repeat the June 1 column, my pastor-dad explained that people in church need to be able to smell their pastor. And what United Methodists call the "means of grace" or "the sacraments" have to involve actual bread and squished grapes and real water. You can't baptize through mime, and you can't feed people the Lord's Supper by telling them to close their eyes and imagine what bread might taste like.

For Christians, incarnation is supposed to be a marker of who we are. Letters can be truly loving, even emailed ones. Photos can be crucial for telling real or pretend stories. Characters on screen or page can be balm when you are lonely. But Christians have at the epicenter of our faith that there is no substitute for the real thing called together.

I have stirred up some classrooms by asking whether students grew up thinking cops are their friends or were warned by elders that a stranger could use police officers against them. The last few months have made it clear to people who do not have friends who are black or Hispanic that this difference involves race. In response, some local news outlets have reported on cities spending gazillions to put cameras on every police officer's head. Those cities have given up on the real thing called together. The image that comes to my mind is from a dystopia called *City of Lost Children*.

Answering the pervasive dehumanization of racism with the further automation of police officers is to live in a logic that is the opposite of incarnate solidarity. It is to accept alienation as reality. As a Christian, I cannot abide that.

In case you are not Christian, and you need another reason to refuse, please consider two things. First, clear-as-day footage cannot mend the cracks fracturing a city. New Yorkers can tell you that. Surveillance technology is a sterile gimmick, at best, when what we need is more transparent, embodied, committed communication with neighbors who live as strangers. Second, repeatedly in American history people who benefit from inequality have divided working people hue from hue by pitting us against one another. This "let's you and them fight" strategy is tried and true and evil. Making cops into machines is clever, and wrong. Durham can do better.

P.S. Durham police officers were fitted for cameras on their helmets. Emergency Medical Technicians in town are being fitted for riot gear. I continue to work and write and pray for otherwise.

I had not read the *Golden Compass* series until preparing to write on the books by Phillip Pullman. The evangelical mainstream in the US had eventually come around on the *Harry Potter* series, with voices declaring that series to be satanic mostly drowned out by evangelical writers finding common ground. It seemed a prudent choice, overall, given that opposing a giant, very successful franchise tends to make you look nutty. But the opposition to Pullman's work has been effectively silencing.

ON GIRLS AND BOOKS

February, 2015

My daughter declared C. S. Lewis a heretic. She was about six, and her father had just read the part in *The Lion, the Witch, and the Wardrobe* where Aslan the lion kills Jadis the witch. She had a sense that readers are to celebrate Jadis's death, and she protested. "But she is a child of God!" We explained to her that, in the Narnia universe, Jadis is *not* a child of God. She is a witch. She is a child of, um . . . Satan. Well, my daughter concluded, C. S. Lewis must not have been Christian, because any Christian knows that every person is a child of God.

Many of the evangelical students I have taught cherish C. S. Lewis. Many of those same students hate the novelist Phillip Pullman. I used to avoid books that were flash points of controversy for conservative students. I did not want to know my own opinion on such books, because I did not want to have an opinion to give if asked. The buzz among many evangelical students was that Pullman intended to replace Lewis's sacrosanct Narnia series with his own paganism. My reaction to the fraught politics of teaching such students was to control carefully what I put in front of my eyeballs. So I simply did not read the Pullman trilogy, His Dark Materials. I only read the first book in the series last year. It was published in North America under the title *The Golden Compass*.

As chance would have it, I read *The Golden Compass* not as an antidote to Lewis's Narnia, but as an antidote to a different book, one by Suzanne Collins called *The Hunger Games*. Last year, a bright young woman wrote a thesis I helped to direct, about dystopian novels written for and about adolescent girls, including *The Hunger Games*. The dozen or so dystopias this student covered have a common thread. All are set in a grisly, futuristic setting where the heroine must learn to kill and/or to die. The plots involve survival or sacrifice in a setting of scarcity and domination. A feminist colleague recommended Pullman's His Dark Materials series to us as a helpful contrast. Bravery in the Pullman series is not about becoming titanium. Instead, courage involves the adventure of using one's creative wits and of recognizing one's desire. A significant point of the Pullman series is the power of awakening, adolescent sexuality.

Pullman diagnoses a problem in Western Christianity. The plot of his series involves an ingenious conceit. In the heroine's world, the part of a person's soul that animates a person is, literally, a companion animal. And the really scary people in the series learn to sever a person from within, pulling apart the animating core of a person in order better to control them. This imaginative scenario allows Pullman to describe graphically how a person can be psychologically dismembered. He also links wholeness with the capacity of a girl, during adolescence, to recognize her own sexual desire. This is the part of Pullman's series that caused such a hullabaloo for some Christians, and it is precisely that part of the third book in the series that some censors in North America had excised. The point at which the heroine starts to connect her sexuality to "the key to a great house she hadn't known was there, a house that was somehow inside her" was significantly clipped for some North American versions.

Reading Pullman and the reactions to him helped me understand my self-censorship in reaction to young conservatives around me, a reaction I have come to call a "corset of the mind." I have become more adept at understanding other Christian women around me who cordon off parts of their soul, or who have had parts of their imagination stunted during adolescence because they were told their desire is a source of danger. C. S. Lewis's

Narnia series remains acceptable to many evangelicals because it is fundamentally prepubescent. A world where witches are bad and must die fits better with today's evangelical mainstream than a world where witches have something to teach girls about sexuality. This all has me wondering why more Christians have not criticized *The Hunger Games* and other contemporary dystopias. Why haven't more Christians rejected a premise of scarcity and a prescription of brutality for our daughters? Is it because we believe in a story of competition, scarcity, and strength? Would we rather our daughters be bulletproof than be in touch with their best wisdom about their bodies and their desires? Is this why there is not a Christian kerfuffle about these large-scale displays of death? The real adventure I myself wish for my students and my daughters is the considerable adventure of knowing themselves well, body and soul.

P.S. I discovered after this piece came out that many readers did not even know the Pullman series exists. It is as if his words were so dangerous that some Christians circled the wagons to keep him out altogether. I here recommend the books, and his ideas, as a way for some Christians to see themselves more clearly. He has spoken important truth about how Christianity shapes the self-perception of girls and women.

This post was prompted by a student. Over a decade ago, a student in my class took my suggestion that some people need to bake themselves fresh cookies every day for Lent. My point was that some pastors and public figures are very keen on abstinence for the masses, while people are not masses. People are each individuals, with particular challenges. And some of the people I know find it difficult to believe that God wants goodness for them. For a person who finds it almost impossible to comprehend that God wishes them to flourish, not suffer, eating their favorite foods during Lent can be a spiritual practice toward healing. The truth of this was reinforced years later, when this student wrote me to thank me for my words. God had used fresh cookies to help her. She had recently told her senior pastor—her boss—that his sermon on fasting for the whole congregation was misguided. He thought she was shirking her responsibility, and probably also did not take kindly to a young woman correcting his senior pastor self. But she is a minister elsewhere now, probably baking cookies for parishioners.

GIVING UP FOR LENT

March, 2015

Lent is a time during the Christian year when many Christians note daily how God repetitively saves us. Lent can be a time for individual, careful reflection about where and when we are cruel to ourselves and where and when we are deeply mistaken about ourselves. It can be a time to inquire prayerfully about ways that a human life can become trapped in prosaic or original forms of evil.

But Lent has become, in some Christian circles, a way of marketing self-improvement—a Christian version of a "New Year's resolution." This version has become distilled to a very basic question: "What are you giving up for Lent?"

My daughter has asked me this question three years in a row. We are United Methodist. The United Methodist Church in North Carolina is following various trends, in an attempt to reclaim our cultural legitimacy. Perhaps due to mega-church growth in the region, some high profile pastors have been trying to find ways to make our brand of mainline Protestantism more compelling. Some influential pastors and youth leaders have been encouraging practices of Lenten abstinence.

This has confused some older United Methodists, who are pretty clear that Protestants do not do such things, if for no other reason than that we would not want to be mistaken for Roman Catholics. But the push to have Lent be a time for self-improvement has caught on with younger Methodists. There is talk in evangelical publishing about how shallow and greedy young people are today. This talk is about as true as "Professor" Harold Hill's warnings about pool halls, but, nonetheless, embracing austerity has become cool for some young Christians. The trend dovetails with other marketing fads that encourage young adults to distinguish themselves from those other sorts of people who eat fast food or "hoard" or shop at big box stores. So, the Lenten "give up things" thing has caught on.

There are at least three things wrong with the "giving up" version of Lent. First, Lent should not be about making ourselves feel better by making ourselves feel worse. When Lent becomes like a new diet it can become, paradoxically, more about you and your will to fix yourself than about God's daily gift of your uniquely miraculous life. Second, picking just the "giving up" part may make Protestants feel hard-core, but it cherry-picks only one part of a larger set of practices that make sense all together. There are Christian traditions that have always kept Lent, and they practice a complex, traditional arc that leads to Easter, when Christians celebrate Jesus' triumph of life over death and abundance over austerity. Kara Slade, an Episcopal priest, explained to me that their churches always have a bowl called a "stoup," filled with baptismal water, for people to dip their hands into as they leave the sanctuary, to know their bodies are marked for life. "Yes, we are dust," she told her congregation on Ash Wednesday, "but we are beloved dust bound for heaven."

This leads me to a final concern with "giving up" during Lent. I have had too many precious students and friends with anorexia or depression or some other form of self-loathing think that pastors should broadly recommend "giving up" as a one-size-fits-everybody message. I have heard confessions of both women and men whose biggest spiritual challenge is receiving the good news that their particular, individual lives are precious and worth sustaining with daily bread and warmth and some shoes that feel comfortable or even look beautiful on their feet.

The Roman Catholic theologian Thomas Aquinas wrote thousands of pages in the thirteenth century about how Christian virtues involve practices that are very particular to each Christian. There is no one, single, tried and true method for being made holy during Lent, because you and I are singular. We each face detailed, different struggles. Someone who is foolhardy may need to move toward what appears as timidity in order actually to become courageous. Or, take the virtue of temperance, which is a mean between insensibility and voraciousness. Someone who has become insensible to pleasure, due to abuse, may actually need to practice courage during Lent in order to receive the proper mean that is temperance. A child who has been told his life is worthless may need to practice pride, not humility, in order to know love.

Lent can be a time when people practice the truth that we are given our daily bread as a gift of grace. It can be a time when a Christian confesses to God with undaunted honesty the true barriers she faces to trusting abundant life. No one practice can satisfy the nuance of this sacred summons.

P.S. My daughter and I have a yearly joke now about Lent. She asks me what I am going to give up, and I tell her something like "guilt" or "shame." She already knows what I am going to say, so she laughs and tells me some version of "Good luck!" Her youth pastors—people who often do not really understand young people—continue to advise her to give up something. This year she is giving up texting after bedtime. I can live with that.

Being a public intellectual, or a public moralist, means that certain causes will call on you to sign something or be a spokesperson for something. I had a very odd experience several years ago, when an organization was fighting an amendment in North Carolina to ban same-sex marriage. I was asked to go on television to debate the issue with a prominent pastor from Raleigh. Before the event, I was given clear talking points, none of which included the issue of same-sex marriage. Someone with access to fancy polling tactics had decided the amendment could be defeated by talking about anything other than the issue that most mattered. I tried to do as I was told, and it was a miserable experience. I declared afterward that I would never again be a pretty puppet for a cause, at least not on purpose. I warned the young man who asked me to write about this national living wage campaign with this story about the amendment. He was giving me talking points, and I explained that I was happy to ask him for help when I needed it. This is the result.

OUR DAILY BREAD

April, 2015

Workers across North Carolina are organizing for a large event "for 15" on April 15. Please consider filing your taxes a day early so you can join us. The gathering will include women who deliver mail, teenage boys who grill hamburgers, young women who grade papers, and men who change Depends undergarments. What do we have in common? We work caring for people's bodies, souls, and minds, and we take our jobs seriously. We take our jobs so seriously that we expect to be treated with dignity at work. We expect to be treated as people, not as tools, because our work demands that we daily treat other human beings with patience and grace.

Christians pray a prayer commonly known as "the Lord's Prayer," where we ask God to give us each day our daily bread. Each day, Christians are to pray for the bread for that day. This part of the prayer is based on a story in the biblical book of Exodus.

The story is about daily bread, bread that arrives with the dew each morning. The Israelites are in the wilderness, and God promises them a daily bread that turns out to be "a fine flaky substance, as fine as frost on the ground" (NRSV). One of the rules God gives about this daily bread is that the people who gather from each tent must only gather what is required, given the number of people who live in that tent. Another rule is that the daily bread be for that day, not stored and carried over until the next day. The exception to this last rule is the gathering on the day before the Sabbath. The night before the Sabbath, people are able to save the daily bread until the next day. If they try to save the daily bread any other day besides the day before the Sabbath, the leftovers "bred worms and became foul" (NRSV).

Over the centuries, some Christians have taken the materially real part of this story from Exodus and turned it into a spiritual "truth" about our immaterial souls. But the Lord's Prayer is a daily reminder that this daily bread thing is a real thing. My soul is intertwined with my body. To say "bread" is primarily about something vaguely to do only with my "spiritual" side, and not also about the food that allows me to flourish as a human being, is to make a rhetorical move that I was taught to call "gnostic." To say the Exodus story is not about real bread is to mistake me for an angel, who does not need to eat. "Give us this day our daily bread" is about real bodies and real bread. It is about gathering fairly and not taking more than your tent's share. And, if you do take more than your share, and try to hold it over until the next working day, it will become foul. Ill-gotten bread will draw maggots to your tent.

The "for 15" labor organizing effort in North Carolina brings people together whose jobs involve daily bread and real bodies. It also includes graduate students and other scholars whose work is often exploited as being "its own reward," as if people who grade papers and teach medieval history do not also need our daily bread. I love reading and writing, but I cannot eat words. The common thread that connects us is that our work requires us to treat other people with dignity, even in undignified scenarios. The young woman who takes your order at the drive-through may have stayed up all night with her colicky baby, but she has to stay calm while you drop your credit card in between the door of your car and your seat. Maybe you were up half the night caring for a terminally ill father. The grandmother who works as a home health care attendant must summon up the kindness to bathe your terminally ill father, even though he sometimes expresses contempt for her. Profound, physical vulnerability does not always bring out the best in people. And if your father's home health care worker is trying to complete her degree at the community college, her teacher needs the wherewithal to take her inchoate questions seriously, and to help quicken her curiosity even when she is discouraged.

All of this work requires that we be paid a truly living wage. All of this work requires that we not be dehumanized at our jobs. North Carolina is proud to be and not just to seem to be. It is our motto. There are some fancy but worm-ridden tents here, and some children going to bed without their daily bread. The "for 15" effort is one good way to fix that.

P.S. The "Fight for 15" effort continues across the United States. At a recent event, held at Duke, many relevant issues were put on the table, except the fact that Duke is the main employer in this area. Basically, we were discussing all sorts of employment, without noting that Duke employs more people in this region than any other single employer. People are scared to talk about their employer. It is part of the reason that all workers need a labor union. Including me.

This began as a sermon. My husband of twenty-one years moved out on Ash Wednesday in 2011. That April, the senior pastor at Trinity UMC, my home church, asked me to preach on Mother's Day. I boldly accepted, and then was frankly terrified. Before I went through divorce, a message that had been going through my head was "I am not the kind of woman who gets a divorce." I finally brought that message to the front of my brain, where I could deal with it, and realized how completely ridiculous this was. I had received message after message through popular media growing up that single mothers are failures, oddities. But my theology of grace was all about God's preference for weird people. So, grace broke the spell of my misery. I was the kind of woman who would go through a divorce. I was brave enough to do this. And then, I climbed up into the pulpit and preached a sermon on Mother's Day. This is very close to what I preached in May, 2011.

MOTHER'S DAY

May, 2015

One friend who served in the military and who does not have children told me that he and his wife avoid church two Sundays every year: Veterans Day Sunday and Mother's Day. He explained that both services are too painful. (I have permission to share this.) Pastors try to broaden Mother's Day, so it is not merely a saccharine ode to "motherhood." But if the second Sunday of May is about Mothers (capital M) at your church, Hallmark has won the day.

The history of Mother's Day is a complicated recipe of sentimentality, commercialism, nationalism, and, believe it or not, feminism. Nineteenth-century abolitionist and feminist Julia Ward Howe was a keen advocate for a national day of motherhood. You can find her 1870 document "Appeal to Womanhood Throughout the World," in a Library of Congress digital collection of broadsides. Her proclamation begins:

Again, in the sight of the Christian world, have the skill and power of two great nations exhausted themselves in mutual murder. Again have the sacred questions of international justice been committed to the fatal mediation of military weapons. In this day of progress, in this century of light, the ambition of rulers has been allowed to barter the dear interests of domestic life for the bloody exchanges of the battle field. Thus men have done. Thus men will do. But women need no longer be made a party to proceedings which fill the globe with grief and horror. Despite the assumptions of physical force, the mother has a sacred and commanding word to say to the sons who owe their life to her suffering. That word should now be heard, and answered to as never before.

Predicting that wars of expansion into the West would continue, and that wars between the colonial powers in North America were only gathering steam, Ward Howe sought to unite women to advocate for an end to violence, "In the name of womanhood and of humanity, I earnestly ask that a general congress of women . . . be appointed and held . . . to promote . . . the amicable settlement of international questions."

This sense that "the mother," as she words it, has "a sacred and commanding word to say" on international politics is a different form of feminism than might be familiar to some readers. Ward Howe was writing out of a tradition that considered women not equal to, but morally superior to men. Women writers and activists during the nineteenth century did not always specify whether what they considered a "feminine" proclivity toward peace was due to physiology or enculturation, but they were clear that this tendency should be a concerted force for real world political change.

Ann Marie Reeves Jarvis was born thirteen years after Julia Ward Howe, and her aspirations were more local. Jarvis was the daughter of a Methodist minister in Virginia and is best known as the mother for whom Mother's Day was founded. A few years before the bloodbath that was the Civil War, Jarvis had started Mothers' Day Work Clubs—groups of women working across Appalachia to organize for better health care. Most salient in this story is how, during the Civil War itself, in the contested region that became West Virginia, many of these Mothers' Day Work Clubs refused to declare allegiance to either side of the war. They continued their work of solidarity and healing across one of the most fundamental battle lines in human history.

It was Ann Jarvis's daughter, Anna Marie Jarvis, who went on a public crusade for "Mother's Day" as a national holiday, with Woodrow Wilson declaring it so in 1914. Before a decade was out, however, Anna Marie became disgusted by ways that the greeting card, floral, and confectionery industry had co-opted her own mother's day. She had hoped to memorialize her mother's dignity, and found the trappings tacky. The odd twist to all of this, in my mind, is that Anna Marie Jarvis had already shifted the holiday, by changing the apostrophe from after to before the "s." Her mother had established "Mothers'" groups, but Anna Marie wanted a day to commemorate each individual's mother, with her own mother at the center—hence Mother's Day. A more predictable tangle in the tale is that Woodrow Wilson encouraged people to commemorate Mother's Day by showcasing the American flag. Worshipers and picnickers were to remember all that mothers had sacrificed as their sons died in war.

I am not against pie, picnics, flowers, or shiny boxes of candy. Let the sugary stuff that is now Mother's Day soon begin. But on the Monday afterward, as a proper emetic, please read Ward Howe's broadside. And pray for an end to the insanity that is war.

P.S. A historian named Amy Kaplan has written on what she calls "Manifest Domesticity." She writes that the idea of two separate spheres for men and women—the political sphere and the domestic sphere—is nonsense. From the books that good citizens are supposed to read to their children to the kind of milk we are to buy, what happens inside an apartment or home is all intertwined with politics. In this piece, I tried to explain that for a general readership. Truly, most of my work is inspired by Amy Kaplan's insight. I do not know how to comment on "capitalism" or "economics" or any other "topic" within political theology without pulling the "topic to be discussed" into real homes, including my own. Perhaps it is important especially to sort out the politics of your home, before you try commenting on other people's homes.

LYING, TRUTH, AND CREATIVITY

June, 2015

One of the joys of teaching is watching a student connect to a gift they did not know they had. In my sixteen years as a teacher, I have seen this happen to people in their late teens and to people in their eighties. Some part of their soul opens up—a new space within them that they did not know was there, and they discover a new love for poetry, painting, or (yes, this sometimes happens) theology. I have also watched as a person shuts off a part of their soul that they were just beginning to see. You can watch this happen on a person's face, as they harden internally to refuse the possibility of knowing something new.

One of my favorite texts about truth is by a North African bishop named Augustine. He wrote a treatise against lying that helps people think about different forms of lying. Some people think there is one definition of a lie. A lie occurs when a person intentionally says something other than what they think is true. A lie is an on-purpose falsehood. This is a useful start. Augustine explains that such lying divides a person. But he goes deeper than this. He writes about how lies can involve a collective agreement to be stupid. People can together tell lies to one another about the past or the present, about a government or a family or any discernable entity to discuss. Lying can become a pattern of willed unseeing. This also divides people from within, because human beings were created to want to seek truth together. It is a basic component of real friendship—to seek new ways to understand ourselves and the world. Augustine says that when we walk around lying we split ourselves from within and block true friendship.

A friend told me to read Jane Smiley's 1995 academic satire *Moo* when I came to North Carolina. The book is set in a fictional university in the Midwest, and one of the plots (spoiler alert) involves a giant research hog in the basement of one of the university's buildings. The friend who recommended *Moo* said I needed to know that every university has a giant hog hidden in the basement. What is literal in Smiley's satire is symbolic for ways that a region's economy shapes the questions teachers and students ask. A trick for surviving at a major research university is to remember there is a giant hog in the basement, and to know that the hog often defines what counts as research. Granted, it is unseemly to *talk* about the hog in the basement. Mostly, we are supposed to make sure the hog keeps getting fatter without openly acknowledging the hog.

Some young adults in Durham are using a buzz word to describe their friends—the "creative class." A man named Richard Florida made the phrase into a thing. Young adults in North Carolina are using the phrase to name one component of our region's burgeoning economy. I am not very creative, but here is something I know. You cannot be creative if your body and soul are split. If you are walking around in a haze of collectively intentional stupidity you will not be creatively creative. Maybe another image will help. If you are participating in the repetitive construction of a box in which to think, you will not be very good at thinking outside that box. Or, to connect *Moo* here, if your energy is spent either ignoring the hog or feeding the hog, you will have scant energy left to be creatively creative.

Two major industries in this region depend on the kind of lying Augustine warns about. First, war. People who serve or who have served in warfare will openly tell you that the work requires a kind of internal split. Training people to kill other people requires a habituation away from what makes human beings human. Add to this the fact that the war in Iraq has involved a giant collective lie we were told and that we told ourselves. There were no weapons of mass destruction in Iraq. This is a fact that everyone must reckon with but that is almost unbearable to face. Second, drugs. Teaching Augustine's treatise against lying in churches across the Triangle has taught me that too many people working in the pharmaceutical industry hate their jobs. They went into medical research to save lives, but too much of their souls are spent spinning new schemes to make money. Teaching and learning creatively will require people in North Carolina to talk about these and other truths and lies. A "creative class" in North Carolina cannot dance blithely on top of the giant hog.

P.S. One gift of teaching in congregations across North Carolina, as a small woman who listens fairly well, is that people have told me their problems before and after I teach. I sometimes receive long emails in response to what I have taught. I have learned so much about what people are struggling with at work, especially from people who seem to be "successful" at work here in this state. This essay felt slightly like I was outing people who had told me their frustrations about work, even though I never share a story without permission. This is one of those essays that made me feel queasy, which usually means I need to keep typing and send it before I chicken out.

The smart Southern friend I do not name here is Lauren Winner. I had read Lillian Smith's *Killers of the Dream* in college, but I had forgotten all about it. As the saying goes about languages, "use it or lose it." Lillian Smith's words had not been part of my necessary vocabulary, so I had forgotten her, mostly. Then I started teaching in the South. There are days when I wonder if I will ever understand my new home. This is not necessarily a negative, given that I enjoy a good mystery.

A HOUSE DIVIDED

July, 2015

Jesus' words about a divided household are so well known that a popular North Carolina bumper sticker refers to them in passing. Jesus talks about the ruin of a divided people in the middle of an argument about whether his healing miracles are miraculous or demonic. Jesus is, of course, clear that he is healing people with the power of the Holy Spirit, not through the power of Satan. This is also the passage where Jesus specifies that the only unforgivable sin is speaking against the Holy Spirit. It is a dense and scary passage, in part because the specific parameters of the one absolutely unforgivable sin are unclear. The concept of a divided house is easy to understand, however. That a divided household cannot hold itself together makes logical sense.

When I started teaching Christian ethics in the South sixteen years ago, I had to learn the hard way that I had no idea what I was talking about. I knew six different languages and had written a book about a Danish philosopher, but I knew very little about what it means to talk about race in the South. The first time I stated, as a simple matter of what I thought to be common sense, that "everyone who grows up in the United States grows up learning how to be racist," I was confused that several students were deeply offended. I learned eventually that some white southerners see racism as a marker of class. As in, *those* tacky white people over *there* are racist. *We* educated white people over *here* are not. And

81

then a smart southern friend recommended I read Lillian Smith's 1949 book on the South: *Killers of the Dream*. The book shifted a part of my soul.

Smith loved the South enough to dig into the intertwined roots of white masculinity, sexual anxiety, and racist terrorism. She taught me to ask white students to risk talking to one another about whether and when they had received "the talk" about just who they were and who they were not allowed to fall into abiding love with. There are different ways to sort how the Confederate flag came to be padlocked at full-mast in South Carolina, and, in *Killers of the Dream*, Lillian Smith explains that this has to do with what she calls "The Lessons." The lessons are taught by a "teacher" that you cannot argue with, because she cannot be literally seen: "These ceremonials in honor of white supremacy, performed from baby-hood, slip from the conscious mind down deep into muscles and glands and become difficult to tear out." Because a significant part of the dance regards who is allowed to have sex with whom, and white men with land and money are at the top of that hierarchy, white men without land and money have rituals to reinforce the lie that they have true freedom. To fly the Confederate flag at half-mast would visually signal something that the flag is specifically supposed to conceal. White men without money and power do not have control over their own bodies, and they were sent shamelessly off to the slaughter to protect an evil economic system from which they did not themselves benefit.

That is the truth that shifted my soul. Lillian Smith wrote about "Two Men and a Bargain," in which she tells the story about how white men who owned land and factories in the South made a bargain with white men who worked on land and in factories in the South:

> Once upon a time, down South, Mr. Rich White made a bargain with Mr. Poor White. He studied about it a long time before he made it, for it had to be a bargain Mr. Poor White would want to keep forever. It's not easy to make a bargain another man will want to keep forever, and Mr. Rich White knew this. So he looked around for

something to put in it that Mr. Poor White would never want to take out.

By this arrangement, Mr. Poor White could pretend to have control over schools, churches, libraries—which children could go where, which hymns would be sung, and which books could be read or burned. This semblance of control was conditional. Mr. Poor White must never, ever stop hating and terrorizing African American men for long enough actually to realize that they are all being exploited, treated as mere cogs in Mr. Rich White's farms and factories. It was a bargain set up meticulously to keep house divided from house and neighbor from neighbor. The South was set up to be like a house divided. It is the carefully arranged opposite of solidarity. Unlike the one unforgivable sin, we can turn around this arrangement. The bargain must end.

P.S. I was overjoyed to hear from people in my church that this essay prompted them either to look up Lillian Smith for the first time or to turn again to her words. If these essays prompt even one new insight into a forgotten author, they are worth the tea it took to keep me typing.

This essay came from a place of righteous anger. I have been teaching recovering evangelicals so long that I had come to internalize self-censorship about even the claim that censorship happens. Anytime I tried to name how young people are influenced by the media, I received push-back from truly gifted students in the class. It seemed insulting to them that I would imply that what they had been watching on their screens or reading in their churches was sometimes skewed to distract or disorient them. They might have been brought up with a notion that "worldly" culture could mess up their lives, but that was limited to what women might or might not wear while dancing in the half-time Super Bowl show or what men might or might not watch when masturbating. I am so grateful for students who pushed back when I tried to explain how "worldly" culture is a complicated mechanism. They have helped me to be brave and, hopefully, to be a bit clearer about what I meant to say.

CONSPIRACY

August, 2015

There is a postcard on my office door with a portrait of President Eisenhower alongside a quote from his departing speech in 1961, during which he used the phrase "military-industrial complex": "In the councils of government, we must guard against the acquisition of unwarranted influence, whether sought or unsought, by the military-industrial complex." Eisenhower spoke of a "potential for the disastrous rise of misplaced power" and of the "economic, political, even spiritual" ramifications of a society structured perpetually by defense. He used the words "total influence" to describe the shift he had seen during his presidency. You can read the speech on the Eisenhower Presidential Library website. I am making a small, tinfoil hat to tape on Eisenhower's head for the postcard on my door. By the definition of the term among some of my younger students, Eisenhower was a "conspiracy theorist."

I am thinking about making a floral tinfoil hat to wear while teaching about war. "Communist." "Fascist." "Socialist." Sweeping dismissals of a politically loaded question function differently depending on the setting and generation. For too many young, white, evangelical Christians, the sweeping dismissal of choice today is "conspiracy theorist." I encountered this in the classroom when asking people to consider which country music stars and songs were highlighted during awards ceremonies in 2002, to name one instance. Even asking some students to think about how the music industry works ended up with my explaining patiently that, yes, people do sometimes "conspire." It was not mere coincidence that jingoistic and/or sentimental war ballads were constantly in our ears that year.

I would not be so troubled if this willed naiveté were isolated. When I hear a commentator on NPR calmly dismiss a complex, geopolitical analysis of the debt crisis in Greece as "conspiracy mongering," I know this is not just a problem among recent graduates of Christian colleges. Here is another example. Pulitzer Prize-winning journalist Seymour Hersh wrote in 1969 about the conspiracy to keep the tragedy in My Lai, Vietnam a secret. He has not let up since, trying to track how lies function. Hersh was asked recently in an NPR interview how he feels when dismissed as crazy. His May essay for the *London Review of Books* challenges the official story on the death of Osama bin Laden, and the recurrent charge that Hersh is psychologically off-kilter came back around in the mainstream media. God bless him, Hersh took it all in stride, apparently. Accustomed to being labeled a loon whenever challenging an official story about war, Hersh told media analyst Bob Garfield that he could not care less whether he is "liked." "When you are running stories that counter the narrative," he explained, journalists who "bought—hook, line and sinker" the standard story will not necessarily thank you for pointing out their fishy gullibility.

Not long after Eisenhower sounded his warning about the "military-industrial complex," John F. Kennedy spoke in his 1963 Commencement Address at American University of the dangers of perpetual warcraft: "Let us examine our attitude toward peace itself. Too many of us think it is impossible. Too many think it unreal. But that is a dangerous, defeatist belief. It leads to the conclusion that war is inevitable—that mankind is doomed—that we are gripped by forces we cannot control." Four years later, Martin Luther King Jr. described a "society gone mad on war," likening the war in Vietnam to "some demonic destructive suction tube" and naming the "brutal solidarity" of black and white boys sent "eight thousand miles away to guarantee liberties in Southeast Asia which they had not found in southwest Georgia and East Harlem." King did not name this as a jumble of coincidences. He named this the "cruel manipulation of the poor."

The use of the label "conspiracy theorist" is an insidious trend. To dismiss someone as nutty because they are asking questions about opacity, money, and power is to leave us with shallow thinkers who give simple diagnoses and palatable solutions— "thoughtful" conservatives and "practical" liberals. The etymology of "radical" relates to the word "root," and I am hungry for both radical journalism and transparent, open collaboration to counter the standard narratives about war in the US. This requires a willingness to question the elevator music that plays in our heads, whether we are watching Fox News or MSNBC. Collaboration will involve open conversation between people who are young enough to question everything and old enough to have lamented My Lai, between people who know intimately the "cruel manipulation of the poor" during perpetual war and those who cannot bear the question. This can happen at the farmers' market or your Bible study. Think of it as a sustained story corps effort, for truth.

This is one essay where I was meddling. I had hoped that I could use my local press stump speech to shape policy at Duke Divinity School. Nothing happened. As of this edit, we still do not have safe spaces for students who are LGBTQ, or their allies. A few years ago, a student took up the charge to designate our hallways as leisure space, through his "Divinity Couch Initiative." Soon afterward, we had some pews in the hallways, so people could actually sit down and visit after class. He was not credited with this change, but I try to remind people that his courage actually changed things—practical things like sitting down in a hallway. I hope that, eventually, we will have space at Duke Divinity School designated for gender-minority students. Because, here where I teach and live, there are fewer and fewer gender-minority students who even recognize themselves in the mirror.

SANCTUARY

September, 2015

Professors are characters. This is a reason the Harry Potter fantasy rings true. Whether teachers in a haunted institution start out strange, many of us grow into characters. When I arrived at Yale Divinity School in 1990, the portraits on the wall might as well have been enchanted, for all the stories swirling around. One history professor had stepped into a trash can while lecturing on Luther, and evidently did not miss a beat. A Bible professor had read straight through the same lecture twice in a row. He did not pause to look up to see his room full of students looking back at him, pens down, amused.

A favorite story is of a beloved teacher named Margaret Farley, a Sister of Mercy who was the first woman on regular faculty in 1971. We were told Margaret Farley had staged a "sit-in" in one of the restrooms in the Divinity library. Yale Divinity School had been admitting women for generations, but there was only one restroom in the school not marked "Men," and no restrooms for women in the library. So, Margaret Farley and several other women sat down in one of the library restrooms, insisting they would not leave until the sign was changed.

Duke Divinity School is also replete with tales of eccentricities and everyday heroism. As the long struggle for civil rights in the South became a televised, national reckoning with racial terror, faculty members at Duke Divinity School pushed vocally for the desegregation of Duke University. In 1948, Divinity students wrote a petition urging Duke University to admit African American students, a "gradualist" process that led eventually to Duke admitting African American undergraduates in 1963. (Duke was one of the last major universities to desegregate.) My colleague Professor William Turner graduated from Trinity College in 1971, and some of us ask him still to tell about faculty members who held other colleagues to account for what might be politely called "quietism." One such professor was Dr. Frederick Herzog. Dr. Herzog died during a faculty meeting in 1995, so I did not have the honor of meeting him. He seems to have been Duke Divinity's Professor Dumbledore, calling other teachers and their students to be courageous, even in their own hallowed hallways. Duke Divinity School was the first seminary in the US to require every student preparing for ministry to take a course in Black Church Studies, and, due to the tireless witness of some, we still do. In the early 1970s, intrepid women at Duke Divinity began a Women's Center, and the newly configured Divinity buildings now include a Women's Center and, thanks to the after-hours mischief of a few colleagues, a hospitality space for children.

Duke Divinity School needs a new Room of Requirement, and one that shows up on every map (that is a Harry Potter reference). In addition to our chapel, with crystal clear windows that open up to the trees, and our inviting, fair-trade and locally grown café, we need a hospitality space for students who are lesbian, gay, bisexual, transgender, or queer. As one coworker put it, we need a designated space that "does not need to be negotiated at any given moment," because "sexual minority students already have to do a lot of negotiating day in and day out." Much as I might wish that LGBTQ students would not need safe sanctuary in the midst of a divinity school, according to them, they do. By naming even a cozy space for the LGBTQ Divinity group "Sacred Worth," the school could witness to students across the university that some Christians affirm the God-created beauty and dignity of "sexual minority students." Given that much of the disapproval aimed at students who are LGBTQ comes from people who profess Christ, a designated space at the professional school that trains people for Christian ministry would send an important message of welcome across the university.

Duke Divinity School is one of thirteen seminaries founded by and sustained by the United Methodist Church. The United Methodist Church officially recognizes the "Sacred Worth" of LGBTQ people, but we do not officially as a denomination yet recognize the sacred calling to ordained ministry of LGBTQ people. That will change. In the meantime, I see no need for our blessed United Methodist ties to prohibit hospitality space. We currently welcome faculty and students to this United Methodist school who speak from Christian traditions that do not recognize the ordination of women, a standpoint that goes manifestly against the long Methodist witness for women's ordination. To be blunt, Duke Divinity School currently welcomes people who are confessedly non-egalitarian, but we do not have one single "out" LGBTQ faculty member. The symbolism of "Sacred Worth" space could reverberate through our historied hallways, changing the stories to come.

P.S. I wrote this essay with young students in mind. But one woman was very concerned when she read this essay. Evidently Harry Potter is still a generational phenomenon. One woman who read this when it appeared in the *Durham Herald-Sun* thought that I was insulting the late Fred Herzog by comparing him to Dumbledore. She did not know the reference, and, to be fair all around, "Dumbledore" was a very clever choice on J. K. Rowling's part. She named him a name that, when read without context, makes him sound "Dumb" and "Boring." Dumbledore is neither. I am so grateful that the woman who took (rightful, if mistaken) offense at my characterization mentioned this to a friend, and that this friend helped her to know that Dumbledore is the hero of the series. He is the kind of scholar who took his position so seriously that he was willing to be misunderstood for the truth.

I was nearly escorted out of a recent Superman movie because I was muttering to myself and my beleaguered date about how horrible the movie was. I have watched so many films about superheroes now that I want a medal, or a Wonder Woman amulet of power, or something. But, truly, watching all of these movies has helped me to better understand how men and many women in my classes have been shaped by what they watch in theaters.

I DON'T NEED ANOTHER HERO

October, 2015

One upside to writing about masculinity is that going to the movies counts as research. I have taught enough men ages 18–35 to know that I need to see every superhero movie. Even if they do not themselves like superhero movies, blockbusters end up being an assumed topic of conversation with their friends and co-workers. One very gracious student who loves superhero movies stayed in conversation with me as I watched hours and hours of backlogged movies. After sorting through the nuances of each era's Superman, the various Batmans, the Spider-Man from *Electric Company* to the Spider-Man crawling up buildings today—I realized I was not going to find a superhero franchise that I like. I was on a fool's errand, because I disagree with the whole shtick.

My mother loves superhero movies, and she has told me she would prefer I keep my holiday film criticism to myself, thank you very much. At the risk of ticking off more loved ones, here is why I do not like superhero movies. They assume that we, the people, need a hero. As one current student pointed out, even the Avengers franchise, which features a team of heroes working together, creates a post-9/11 feedback loop. Each film features teeming groups of humans, running around like scattered ants, on the verge of mass destruction, needing a team of superhumans to save us from the forces of chaos. He astutely observed that our repetitive viewing of impending chaos keeps people trapped in a trauma response to 9/11. He suggested that we end up stuck feeling afraid, and saved, and afraid, and saved—usually by a man who can do something we are fundamentally unable to do. Merely mortals, without Batman's fortune or Superman's genes, viewers watch ourselves saved from apocalypses. I suppose there are some viewers who leave the movie theater inspired to put on a superhero suit and save someone, but that is also a fool's errand. Trying to be someone else's savior is a very bad idea, however cute the suit and however pretty the damsel.

In case someone thinks that Iron Man is the exception (I hear this frequently) please consider how the ironic twist of those movies depends still on a man-saving-the-world template. Though the perky woman next to him puts on a similar superhero costume, the overarching assumptions of the superhero story remain intact. We, the people, cannot manage ourselves. We, the people, are under threat from this or that form of villainy. We, the people, need a hero. This is a profoundly undemocratic way of seeing the world. I am baffled that filmmakers get away with this unpatriotic stuff. But they do get away with it, and the superhero stench wafts over into other genres. From Lincoln to Martin Luther King Jr., historical dramas have recently offered filmgoers a grand story of a great man who was able to make history. In his review of Spielberg's reconstituted Lincoln, David Bromwich sums up beautifully what is wrong: "Any leader who adopts the posture of *seeing himself on the stage of history* is a glory to himself and a menace to all whom he must lead." Even Atticus Finch was not, it turns out, Atticus Finch. Whatever you make of the controversy around or the quality of Harper Lee's *Go Set a Watchman*, the take-away message is that Gregory Peck's 1962 depiction of the character is satisfyingly lacking in subtlety. Life together is not a superhero movie.

Democracy depends on cacophony—on the discord of disparate voices. Hero narratives assume cacophony is a problem to be overcome, whether by a man in a cape or by a great speech given by a great man on a big stage. Craving a leader who stands above me is an impulse I must resist, if I am going to be a citizen in a democracy or even if I am just going to be a constructively critical human being. Or, if I am going to remain Christian. Churches sometimes crave a hero as much as Fox audiences (evidently) crave a big Reagan airplane. When we do, we should read and read again the beginning of Acts, when the church receives a very different kind of power. People who were not supposed to speak to one another, or speak up at all, talked all at once. Writing during a time of famine, the Hebrew prophet Joel had seen a vision of a miracle whereby women and even servants would speak up. The beginning of Christianity depends on that vision. That is reason enough for me to resist the temptation to find a hero.

P.S. A student who asked me to supervise his final project on superheroes wrote me after this was posted to tell me that this essay helped him better to understand the ways he had been taught to see himself. That is worth the price of all the bother.

This essay is a follow-up to the essay on pornography. Somehow, the way I had written about pornography had captured all the attention, and not my objection to online education. I continue to observe that "online education" is an oxymoron. Meaning, it is possible to learn things from the Internet. That is true. But it is not possible to receive an education while looking at a screen. Jesus came in the flesh. If we do not confess this as true, as Christians, then we might as well go ahead and be something else. I am fine with that, but I am not fine with pretending to be Christian and advocating for formation online. To be clear, I would prefer you share this essay in person, over some good food or during a long walk through the city or the woods. In other words, I think it is possible to learn from a book. But a book shared is much better than a book kept alone, or "starred" in a review.

LEARNING DEPENDS ON TIME TOGETHER

November, 2015

My daughter has been texting all weekend. She has respected my rule not to text during worship, meals, or late at night. Even within these guidelines, I find myself talking like a Saturday Night Live character named the Grumpy Old Man. The Grumpy Old Man skit involved Dana Carvey describing the good old days, when children did not have confounded cell phones. Throwing up my hands in frustration, I did what any modern mommy does. I turned to the Internet. Watching the musical number "Telephone Hour" from the 1963 hit *Bye Bye Birdie* made me feel better. What did we do before cell phones? We tied up our household's landline for hours, talking about vastly important teen crushes. At least I did.

I relate the story above, about telephones, in part to reassure readers that I am not against all technological communication. Most of the time, I am not a caricature of the Grumpy Old Man. But, when a friend told me recently that the future of pedagogy is online education, I vowed to resist. I am as opposed to this form of the future as I would be if a friend told me that the future of sex is online, or that the future of worship is online, or that the future of our friendship is online. Learning—like friendship, worship, or sex—is a gift best shared with other human beings, face-to-face. A song from the musician Red Grammar puts it well: "It's as simple a thing as the air that we breathe; we need time together."

A school can avoid paying teacher salaries and basic benefits if it moves toward distance education. This is the ostensible reason that children in Durham are "taking classes" online, with someone, somewhere, answering their typed-in questions. Money is also the ostensible reason that Christians are working online for degrees through my own institution. We sit in front of a computer, Skyping, which means that we awkwardly see one another on a screen. The display looks sort of like the television game show *Hollywood Squares*. I submit that the loss is not worth the monetary gain. What we lose in online learning is fundamental to the gift of teaching.

I have taught a seminar on a Danish philosopher named Søren Kierkegaard ten times during my sixteen years teaching at Duke. We have read the same books together, each iteration of this seminar, but every semester is different. Classes are made up of people, and people are individuals, with snowflake-unique experiences and perspectives. I learn something new that surprises me every time I teach, even when I am teaching a book for the umpteenth time. A vital part of this gift is the trust that students build with one another over time. The interactions in person matter, as we each let down our guard and risk showing confusion, or insight. Body language matters for teaching. If a student crosses his arms and scowls, I know I need to pause the conversation. Has the conversation left him lost? If he is lost, chances are someone else in the room is also lost, but trying to hide it. This is one obvious example. Good teachers learn to pick up subtle cues, to help each person in the class learn. Even if the class is about information—about facts—the classroom matters. A geometry teacher learns how to teach geometry well by answering questions from befuddled students. She may stay up late thinking about how better to explain a difficult concept and, the next year, she has a new pedagogical trick. I may be able to see consternation on a student's face online, and some confused students will risk typing a question online. But trust is best built minute by minute, session by session, in person.

We may enjoy the polished perfection of a carefully constructed TED Talk on screen, but polished perfection is not the same as teaching live people to whom you are accountable and from whom you are learning. Which brings me back to a question I asked last month in my essay against superheroes. How can online learning be the "future" of education in a democracy? A flourishing democracy requires not only a people filled up with facts, but people who have been formed to learn from one another by listening to distinct voices and hearing particular stories. Sharing the task of learning with people who are different than you are is a hedge against tyranny. This is one reason why we finally desegregated public schools across the United States. Placing each student in front of her own little computer, interacting on screen, is a form of re-segregation. The gift of time together is worth public support in a vigorous democracy.

P.S. To be continued. This is probably the most "train-has-left-the-station" essay in this collection. Unless, of course, people talk to one another and decide otherwise.

This essay started over a make-up counter. One of my post-divorce indulgences was to go have my face made up at Macy's department store. I became friends with two of the women who work there, and we have talked frequently over the last five years about the witness of kindness that people in retail are often called on to give, or not give. Macy's is more racially integrated than my church, and I have found myself in candid conversations there about mothering, clothing, dating, and all sorts of other things that I have not discussed with people at my church of nearly two decades. I wanted to witness to ways that people are both exploited and gifted at shopping malls in the US, and this was one, hopefully winsome, way to complicate the whole "shopping is bad" versus "shopping is good" debate that has happened in the mainstream media for years after Thanksgiving.

"BLACK FRIDAY" IS A MIXED BAG

December, 2015

Before I confirmed a call to ordained ministry, my dad told me something I now tell students preparing for ordained ministry. The life of a pastor can be summed up in one imperative. On Christmas Eve, after the last worship service, make sure every toilet in the church is flushed. This imperative assumes an important fact. The imperative assumes that, on Christmas Eve, the pastor is the only one working. Even though the church may have someone on staff to lock up doors and to care for post-worship tidying, that person will not be working on Christmas Eve. My dad has flushed many Christmas Eve toilets over his half-century of ministry. Such is the glamorous life of an inn keeper at Christmas.

Growing up in a parsonage, Advent involved more than the usual tidying up, as we hosted choir parties, youth parties, and Sunday school parties. The parties were spread out over Advent, so "Christmas" started early. My brother and I sliced sausage rolls and cut crusts off fancy little loaves of bread used only for such parties. We cleaned bathrooms and took out trash and dusted bookshelves, so guests would know we considered them worth the trouble. The timing of these church parties at our house necessitated that Christmas jump the calendar forward to Thanksgiving. We would often put up the tree before Thanksgiving, so everything would be ready when we came back from my grandparents' annual Thanksgiving reunion. Technically, Advent is about anticipation—anticipating the birth of Jesus. But my mother is a practical woman, and she was not about to let a liturgical rule discombobulate the proper ordering of things.

My second home growing up—my home away from home—was the nearest shopping mall. My mother loves shopping malls. A fantastically creative seamstress, she goes to the mall to spark her imagination for unique twists on fashion. She started a Thanksgiving shopping tradition when I was young. Thanksgiving was my father's family's holiday. One set of cousins on that side did not celebrate Christmas, and my father always worked on Christmas Eve, so we would travel each year to Mineral Wells for a Thanksgiving extravaganza. This involved Russell Stover candies, squash casseroles, fried okra, turkey, ham, and at least a dozen pies. After all this cooking and an interminable amount of dishwashing, every woman and girl-child in the family was exhausted. While every man and boy-child sat around watching football Friday after Thanksgiving, those of us who had cooked and cleaned on Thanksgiving escaped to a fancy shopping mall in Ft. Worth. We spent the Friday after Thanksgiving walking under sparkling Christmas lights, looking at neatly arranged clothes—and decidedly *not* cooking or cleaning.

These are the backdrop stories for my assessment of what has come to be known as "Black Friday." This time of year, news and social media sources offer a clashing combination of enticement and shame. "Shop big savings!" advertisements compete with "Shame on greedy shoppers!" op-eds, videos, and photos. News crews take cameras to big box stores, not upscale boutiques. Women who shop in bulk at Costco are not particularly greedy. But they apparently create a better spectacle for moralistic scorn than women shopping at Talbots. And women shopping anywhere are apparently a more effective story about the ungodly spread of rampant consumerism than are men watching football in the living room. I counter that dressing rooms can be a place for sisterly bonding, even with complete strangers. I prefer trying on clothes alongside other real people, with real, non-photoshopped bodies and faces. Malls are more humanizing than shopping on my computer, trying to imagine what a dress on a pretend person would look like on my actual self. There can be a camaraderie of such kindness on "Black Friday." I have seen holy mischief at the mall—the presence of God in the mix of neighbors watching mechanical bears sing "Silent Night," weeks before we are, technically, supposed to celebrate the birth of Jesus.

I have been searching my brain for any possible upside to a new "Black Friday" trend, and I have come up short. Some stores have taken to opening on Thanksgiving night and staying open all night long, jump-starting the holiday season by telling employees to host people all night long. This, I submit, is a story of greed, and not on the part of shoppers. My dad taught me to assume that a good employer does not expect the janitor to work on Christmas Eve. Charles Dickens teaches us that a boss who expects employees to work on an important feast day is headed toward a gloomy fate. Executives who tallied the numbers and opted for the trend of all-night holiday shopping should take another look, in the mirror.

P.S. I preached at my father's church on the Sunday after Christmas, right after this essay went also up on my personal blog. Several people at the cozy church at which he was serving as an interim minister told me that they had offered to flush the church toilets on Christmas Eve for him. I also heard a sweet note from my friend at Macy's, who reiterated that she finds ways to discover joy even on the overnight stint.

A CASE FOR LOCAL, INDEPENDENT JOURNALISM

January, 2016

There are high-tech adventures in theaters to strengthen one's New Year's resolve. Many of them have the word "courage" in the description. I recommend *Spotlight*. It is the most encouraging movie I have seen in forever.

Thomas Aquinas offers a helpful description of courage. This thirteenth-century writer is the authoritative theologian for the Roman Catholic Church. I have learned tricks over years of trying to entice Protestant students to read him. The section of his classic *Summa Theologiae* that hooks students is on virtues and vices. No one parses the fine distinctions between, for example, jealousy and backbiting, or anger and spite, or temperance and insensibility like Thomas Aquinas. It only takes a few years in a real congregation with actual people to note the almost infinite variety of vice and virtue.

Thomas continues in a tradition to treat fortitude (courage) as one of the four basic or "cardinal" virtues. Along with practical wisdom, temperance, and justice, courage is one of four habits of being that orient a person to understand who and where they are, and how their corner of the world fares in relation to the pivotal aspects of life that make life good. To understand what Thomas means by the cardinal, or orienting, virtues, think of the opposite: an intentionally disorienting story. Some writers try intentionally to disorient people, for laughs, or to make life appear utterly random. Such writing can make you temporarily unable to regain your balance. Courage is one of four virtues that may allow a person to regain her bearings. Courage is often necessary to determine what is just, or practical, or temperate, particularly when people with power around you are impractical, intemperate, or unjust. Thomas further explains that each of the four cardinal virtues balance between two excesses. Courage is a habit of being between foolhardiness, on the one hand, and, on the other, living fearfully. Sometimes a person has to cultivate courage in order to point out what is nonsensical.

Or to point out what is obscene. The word *obscene* names something so disorienting that it assaults your senses, rendering you senseless. Here is one local example. Several years ago this newspaper ran an article on how some executives at Duke University had given themselves large bonuses during a period when supposedly everyone at the university needed to "tighten our belts" and do with less. While librarians and surgeons and nurses and teachers were doing much more with much less, some higher-ups received giant gold checks. The week the story broke, one distinguished colleague saw me in our office hallway in a tiara and black velvet dress. He asked me what in the world I was doing. I told him I was on my way to perform street theater to draw attention to the scandal. He shook his head and said, "It really is obscene." He did not go on record, but I used his word *obscene* repeatedly in public to characterize the mess. The most courageous thing I have ever done was declare publicly that my marriage was untenable. The most brazen thing I have done ever was participate in a group effort to whistle blow, at my employer, wearing a tiara. But we would not even have had a whistle to blow without old-fashioned, journalistic muckraking.

In his description of courage, Thomas Aquinas thinks through how courage intertwines with endurance. *Spotlight* relates with similar attention to detail the actual story about a team of journalists with the *Boston Globe* who together discover the courageous patience sufficient to trace a pattern of disorienting deceit. Boston clergy, lawyers, and other public figures sustained a meticulously crafted, multifaceted cover-up of the fact that at least a thousand children had been sexually violated by over a hundred church leaders in the Boston area alone. The film depicts the slow, steady, journalistic tenacity necessary for raking up such stealthily buried muck. The film also shows how a brilliantly lying set of liars can hone the subtle skills of manipulation and intimidation. Each journalist in the story has to develop the courage both to note subtly delivered threats and to continue, even while noting the power behind these threats, the mundane but heroic tasks to expose truth. An important part of the film is how Boston is a "small town," and how a key, regional institution may develop a shield of amoral invisibility. "The Church" had become a given, an indisputable "Good," capital G, both uniting and silencing people. *Spotlight* is in this way a real story comparable to Henrik Ibsen's 1882 play *An Enemy of the People*. Ibsen also relates the stakes of telling the truth in a town living a lie. Both stories vividly show why courageously independent, local journalism is vital for living well.

P.S. If you have not watched *Spotlight*, see it soon! I have been grateful this year for the many courageous people who are boycotting the Oscars due to the dearth of African American nominations year after year after year. This is one film that deserves many Oscars in 2016. *Star Wars* is all over everything as I type this, but *Spotlight* is the movie I want both of my daughters and all of my students to see.

This is my testimony to the need for people to trust, even when there seems ample evidence to the contrary. It is a love letter to readers.

ROLLER COASTER OF LOVE

February, 2016

I stayed up way too late last night following social media about the Iowa Democratic caucus. My house has a pink and blue home-made sign in front proclaiming "The Green Street Girls [Heart] Bernie Sanders." The last time I had this much love in the game was during Obama's first primary run. I remember talking to a good friend in Chicago about the race. He and his son were travel-ing to campaign for Obama across the Midwest. "Do you really think Obama is going to change things?" I asked him, hopeful but also trying to be realistic. "He is going to break our hearts," he said, "but I am campaigning for him anyway."

It is not easy to put your heart back into a game after your heart has been broken. After I went through divorce five years ago, I was talking to a new friend about trusting in love again. He and his wife train horses, and they likened the task to getting back onto a horse after you have been thrown off of one. You cannot let your fear rule you. You have to trust again that the world is more safe than not—that people are more worth loving than not. I have found this to be true not only for trusting in romantic love, but also for trusting a new church after a congregation has thrown you off the horse, so to speak, or for trusting a new classroom after you have gone through a really rough ride with a group of particularly rude students. Investing your heart, truly risking a part of your soul by loving a person or a group of people, can be harrowing. "Nothing ventured, nothing gained" may be true, but it is not easy. To venture a sufficient part of yourself truly to be open to love is scary.

Another friend compared dating after divorce to being in free fall. He is older than I am, and I had confessed that I felt like I was twelve again, and that it was unsettling. He reassured me that he often feels twelve also, and added that he often feels like a twelve-year-old in free fall. Members of funk band the Ohio Players were definitely grown-ups when they wrote their 1976 hit song "Love Rollercoaster." They are singing about loving a sweetheart, and the sense of both exhilaration and barely controlled panic that go along with such love. The writers of the 1989 movie *Parenthood* use the same exact image for what it means truly to be part of a family. The grandmother in the film puts it this way: "You know, it was just so interesting to me that a ride could make me so frightened, so scared, so sick, so excited, and so thrilled all together! Some didn't like it. They went on the merry-go-round. That just goes around. Nothing. I like the roller coaster. You get more out of it."

Richard Thompson has a song that says something similar about love. He wrote it around the same time that his marriage to singer and songwriter Linda Peters was coming apart at the seams. It is called "The Wall of Death," referencing a circular track where people ride a motorcycle or other vehicle sideways, basically. You will have to look up images yourself, because words fail me. I cannot begin to imagine riding a motorcycle sideways. But Richard Thompson sings "you're going nowhere when you ride on a carousel," which is true. Grandma is right. As one saying about family goes, having children means consenting to allow your heart to walk around outside your body. I have seen this be true also for love between sweethearts, and love of children for parents.

Investing your heart with fidelity is not always exhilarating. Putting your heart into a game—venturing, risking, trusting—is also about the tiny little steps that make love possible. Bernie Sanders tied Hillary Clinton in Iowa not due to something giant, but through one little phone call after another, one conversation after another, made with patience, not so much with valor. Love between two sweethearts is similar, like kindling, as one of my favorite television shows put the matter recently. Life together is made little stick by stick. That same series has a very astute argument against couples writing their own wedding vows. In one episode, a young couple writes absolutely ridiculous vows to one another, describing love as an up-front, 100 percent sure sort of thing, thereby confounding other young couples in the congregation. I am grateful the marriage vows in my tradition are set in stone by old people, who, even though they sometimes feel like twelve-year-olds in free fall, know that love is also about getting back on that horse, trusting daily that the world is more safe than scary.

I had written an essay in September, 2015 to make the case that Duke Divinity School needs space designated as hospitality for lesbian, gay, bisexual, transgender, and queer students. By March, 2016, that request had gone unheeded. I wrote this piece to be crystal clear about my perspective, knowing that these words would seem harsh to some. The last paragraph references recent work by well-known and well-promoted Christian writers who use the work of scholar Judith Butler (among others) to promote gender conformity. I had to edit that paragraph to express clarity rather than anger. But I am genuinely angry about this new, very sophisticated, anti-gay effort.

WHY I AM CHRISTIAN AND PRO-GAY

March, 2016

A North Carolina middle school has started a support group for gay students and friends. I celebrate this. Adolescence is a fine time to receive attentive friendship and mentoring about sexuality. My mother was a middle school teacher. She says it's a time when kids begin to get their "stuff" together. (She uses saltier wording around adults.) We begin to sort out how to define our own style of fashion, practice our signature, and discover our gifts for arts or sports at the very time we are trying to accommodate to bodies that shift weekly. It is tricky, finding your own "voice" when your voice cracks while trying to impress a peer. Add to this what can be an isolating realization that your lack of conformity to the predictable Adam and Eve pairing was not just a periodic quirk of elementary school, but a solidifying desire to kiss someone of the same sex.

A friend recently sat through a preschool evaluation of her child that included the question "Are you a boy or a girl?" Her toddler "failed" the test. She wondered how other parents might react to such "failure." Would some children be corrected or scolded for their reply? Adolescence is similar to toddlerhood in that parenting involves a combination of encouragement and caution. You cannot parent a toddler well while constantly shouting "be careful!," "do not run!," and "slow down!" Of course you must teach a child not to run in an unsafe place, but cheering the transition from crawling to walking to running, skipping, and jumping is part of what makes a good parent good. Teaching a toddler they must identify clearly by gender is also a good way to be a bad parent. Similarly, adolescence is a time when adults need to encourage as often as warn. If most of your messages to your middle school child are about the perils of their gender and sexuality, they will learn that their bodies are dangerous. That might or might not keep them chaste. It could leave them unable even to name their own desire.

There are two popular arguments against my case. One is that sexuality is inherently anarchic unless formed with a procreative purpose. There are Christians who believe a fundamental building block of all that makes human society workable is that sex leads to babies. If sexuality is unhooked from making babies, then society itself becomes unhinged from reality. Think of the words to the song "Anything Goes!" and turn it into a sermon. By this reasoning, sexuality needs to be disciplined from early in life, so that each individual understands they are part of a future dyad called man/woman. By this reasoning, if a middle school boy is able without shame to name that he is beautifully and wonderfully made gay by God, then the firmament may fall down on our heads. I affirm that God alone holds up the sky. I also lament the harm this version of conformity has caused people I love.

There are smart people writing critically about a "Prosperity Gospel." I am concerned about a growing "Austerity Gospel." By this form of "Good News," God brings people closer to one another and to God when we are suffering or otherwise helpless. I have heard people living through miserable marriages bemoan the growing, cultural acceptance of gay marriages because "marriage is not about happiness." Read charitably, what they are saying is marriage is more often about forgiveness than pleasure. But an "Austerity Gospel" risks privileging the "worse" part of the "better or worse" vow, as if God wishes for us primarily obedience, and uses our pain. I do not believe suffering leads inexorably or even frequently toward holiness. Just as absence can make a heart grow stranger, suffering can make a heart turn mute.

A few clever writers have come up with a new form of what is called "conversion therapy." They take new affirmations that gender and sexuality are fluid, and use this fluidity to assert that gay people can be happy in heterosexual marriages. If not all people are made to conform to the man/woman binary, this argument goes, then who is to say that a gay or lesbian person cannot be happy in a heterosexual marriage? If "anything goes," then gay Christians are called to go with the will of God, and search until you find someone of the opposite sex who is compatibly gender-bending. This is Christianity at its most insidious. First, raise children not to know themselves and then, if by courage and grace they still identify as gay, use a new form of disorientation toward obedience. Given this foolishness, I can only pray more middle schools will offer support. I pray gay children may grow up to be brave, and joyfully defiant.

P.S. My younger daughter's middle school is the school I had discovered started this support group. Knowing that this essay might invite hate mail, I blurred that fact. I do not mind hate mail, but I did not want my daughter's principal or teachers receiving hate due to my words. I worried over wording in a different way here. I know that the *Durham Herald-Sun* readership is older, and more traditional than I am. So, I was fairly sure that I would lose potentially sympathetic readers if I used a more complicated and therefore true language system for sexual minorities. If, for example, I used the shorthand term LGBTQ, I would lose many readers in confusion. If I explained every word in that shorthand term—specifying lesbian, gay, bisexual, transgender, and queer—I would lose some readers who cannot begin yet to sort out how to understand people whose lives are marked by those last three terms. The term "gay" continues as an umbrella term for all people who are LGBTQ in many circles in the South. So, what I did was a bit awkward. I wrote to friends and family members who are sexual minorities and asked them if my essay was, in balance, more helpful than obfuscating. The response was positive, so I took a deep breath and hit "send." Christian discipleship and local activism are always works in progress . . . .

TRUE POPULISM

April, 2016

The drill team at my high school in West Texas made some un-orthodox song choices for routines. One of them was "Crazy Train" by former Black Sabbath vocalist Ozzy Osbourne. This song has been going through my head during election season. Song-writers Robert Daisley and Randall Rhoads penned: "Crazy, but that's how it goes, millions of people living as foes. Maybe, it's not too late, to learn how to love, and forget how to hate." They go on to name that "heirs of the cold war" are vulnerable to media mes-saging that keeps people living as foes: "The media sells it, and you live the role."

I was recently back in Texas for a wedding. A recurring loop was "No politics!" One patriarch advised, only half-jokingly, if a conversation starts drifting that direction, interject "How about them Cowboys?" A cousin told my daughter, "Whatever you do, don't name the one who shall not be named." Waiting to disembark on the flight home, one hapless neighbor said something about Sarah Palin, and people visibly winced, anticipating an old fight was on. This instant-argument, divide-and-conquer mess now has a name. The term is "dog-whistle politics." Keep people living as foes by crafting a figure so divisive we cannot discuss politics with the people we are supposed to love. "The media sells it, and you live the role." When we cannot discuss our shared future with relatives, something is wrong. Afraid to seem uncivil, or erudite, or backward, or radical, or misinformed, or snooty, we stick to talking about recipes or sports. Some might sweep this into an indictment of "political correctness," but it is a form of political manipulation. We shout at one another on social media but stay silent when together. This is a crazy train.

True populism requires that people who need to work for a living (meaning, like, all of us) actually talk to one another about what we are experiencing as we work or look for work. For starters, try this: "Name a time when you stood up for yourself at work," or "Name a time when you stood up for a co-worker." "Populism" is a phrase political pundits are now using to sort you and me—that is, the populace—and their words are worse than a poor substitute for actual, political conversation with neighbors. Their words are an insulting distraction. The talking heads amplified on media and social media further divide and silence people who need one another to reverse this second great depression.

Here are two examples of insulting distraction. Assessing support for the one who shall not be named, an ostensibly "conservative" media outlet called the *National Review* ran these words: "Even the economic changes of the past few decades do very little to explain the dysfunction and negligence—and the incomprehensible malice—of poor white America." The writer continues, "The truth about these dysfunctional, downscale communities is that they deserve to die." The writer recommends people leave the towns where they grew up and get a U-Haul (with what extra income, I am not sure) to go somewhere else. This is a hateful, unapologetic form of social Darwinism. If you cannot afford to leave home, you deserve to die. Another widely circulated assessment of "populism" from a supposedly "liberal" source was Gloria Steinem's suggestion that young women prefer a labor advocate from Vermont over a hawkish, free-trade proponent because "When you're young, you're thinking: 'Where are the boys?'" Steinem actually said that. In both cases, ways that working people are genuinely struggling to find traction are dismissed as besotted. Either you're clinging to a past best thrown in the trash or you're hoping to date a hipster. What if people privy to these dog whistles talk to each other? What if we get off the crazy train and remember, if not how to love, then at least how to work together?

This essay will appear on Sunday, April 3. I recommend we each bring a neighbor to see *Where to Invade Next* at the Carolina Theatre in Durham. A reviewer named Jon Schwarz writes about the main message of this movie: "You and I aren't bad. All the people around us aren't bad . . . . If regular people get control over their own lives, they'll use it wisely rather than burning the country down in a festival of mindless debauchery . . . . [The movie] is all the more powerful because it doesn't tell you this, it simply shows you. It's not speculation about how human nature will be transformed after the revolution so we'll all be happy to share our ration of grass soup with The People. It's all happening right now, with imperfect human beings just like us." As Ozzy sings, "it's not too late."

THREE SELECT SERMONS

I love to give lectures to groups of people. I especially appreciate the question and answer portion that most groups hold afterward. Sermons are much harder, in my experience, than lectures. People may or may not expect to hear something holy from a person giving a lecture. People are supposed to anticipate something holy to happen when a preacher speaks during worship. Here are three sermons I gave in three different settings. For readers curious about how I speak when I am talking to Christians specifically about God, these may be helpful.

HOMILY ON THE OCCASION OF THE ORDINATION OF KARA NICOLE SLADE TO THE SACRED ORDER OF PRIESTS

July, 2013

St. Stephen's Episcopal Church, Oxford, North Carolina
Texts: Isaiah 6:1–8; Ephesians 4:7, 11–16; John 6:35–38

Christ be with me, Christ within me, Christ behind me,
Christ before me, Christ beside me, Christ to win me,
Christ to comfort and restore me.

Thank you, dear members of St. Stephen's, for your gracious hospitality. Thank you, Bishop Curry and Bishop Hodges-Coppel, for your kindness toward this member of the upstart sect that is Methodism. And thank you, Kara Nicole Slade, for consenting to have your mouth seared with a live coal—for standing up in the middle of swirling seraphs, before the high and holy throne of the Lord and saying, "Here I am."

First to our Gospel reading. Jesus said to them, "I am the bread of life. Whoever comes to me will never be hungry, and whoever believes in me will never be thirsty." I will be frank, the way Jesus speaks in John's gospel annoys me. I find myself thinking that John's Jesus has a problem with tone, using ethereal, holy words that hover way above us, reminding us we are beneath him. The term "imperious" comes to mind. If I am not careful, I hear Jesus speaking of his mission as if he is the honor-bound head butler in a large British manor house. And this passage is one that I find particularly confusing.

No hunger? No thirst?

Christians have and continue to die from quite literal hunger and of lack of potable water. It seems a bit weird and maybe cruel for Jesus to use the words "bread," and "hunger," and "thirst" in so figurative a way that they seem way up here—not connecting to our vulnerable, mortal, food-and-water–dependent bodies.

And, if we do shift upstairs to the realm of ideas, and go along with a more figurative, or symbolic meaning of hunger and thirst, isn't it the case that many Christians do *crave* the shalom of God, the peace of God? Isn't it the case that many people who come to Jesus and eat the bread of life at this table find our hearts transformed such that we *hunger* for peace or thirst for justice? Don't some of us eat this bread of life and discover a new, physiological yearning for more Jesus right here, right now in places near and far?

For a military drone to be transformed into a mother pelican.

For a torn marriage to be stitched miraculously together again.

For a local bank whimsically to overflow with glittering cash for more milk and more honey.

Truly, I don't think Jesus meant that if we come to him we will not be hungry, or thirsty, or else Jesus was a liar, or maybe mistaken. And I don't believe Jesus was a liar or mistaken.

The passage about bodies and grace from Ephesians helps me to begin to say a word about what Jesus may have meant. "But each of us was given grace according to the measure of Christ's gift." Each of us was given grace according to the *measure* of Christ's gift. This word *measure* seems key. How does one reckon the measure of Christ's gift? The word *measure* comes up again, as Paul, the author of Ephesians, connects the different ways we are gifted and called with the "measure of the full stature of Christ." Paul layers metaphors here, so bear with him. The brand new baby church in Ephesus, to whom he is writing, has as its working principle, or its very heart, the "measure of Christ's gift." And so the "whole body" that is their little church is "joined and knitted together by every ligament" he says, through the "measure of Christ's gift." "Apostles, prophets, evangelists, pastors, and teachers" are formed together, joined and knitted into one body, and the organizing principle of their movement, or the DNA of their make-up as a body, is the infinite, never-exhausted grace that is Christ's gift. The central animating fact of the church as a body is immeasurable—not open to study (no matter who is funding it) or to counting or to managerial schemes or to a critical sense of there being not enough. The church moves, according to Paul, in a way that is the opposite of austerity.

Maybe it is from this place, from this incalculable fact of miraculous grace that, though we still find ourselves hungry, we are never totally alone.

I find Paul's list of the different parts of the body here also helpful. In fourteen years of teaching seminarians, I have come to see that prophets are not always so keen to see the gifts of teachers. Teachers are known for parsing different particulars, describing the nuances of discipleship. Prophets would like a little less nuance and a lot more righteousness, thank you very much. And, truth be told, many teachers are not so keen on the annoyingly happy zeal of evangelists. And, pastors can be annoyed by apostles, as a pastor is called to sit still, right here, patient and over time, with one church, while apostles go out gallivanting across the church universal.

Paul describes the body that is Jesus' church as connected and linked in grace, in such a way that we who are different from one another are awesomely stuck with one another, counterintuitively connected together, re-membered in grace and pulled together in something Paul calls love and that Jesus calls life.

In our Gospel passage from John, Jesus tells us "Anyone who comes to me I will never drive away." I think that this is connected to the ways that we will never, truly, ultimately, be alone with our distinct gifts and burdens. The hunger and thirst that is our mortal, yearning life can never ultimately isolate you, or me, leaving us dismembered from the body or cast out. And these two passages, read together, perhaps also testify to the fact that we can never ultimately hide ourselves away, with either our gifts or our struggles. We cannot sit alone, satiated, or starve ourselves from the sustenance that is the bread of Jesus. Could it be that, once we are pulled into the body of grace that is a church, we cannot sustain the spiritual anorexia of despair or the gluttony of lonely ambition? I am not totally sure, but Scripture inspires me to be more sure.

I myself have felt utterly alone before, not only in a pew, but, truth be told, in a pulpit. But grace has, finally, come back drip by drip, almost like an IV, and I don't realize I have been linked back into the body until I am no longer so devastatingly parched.

Kara, as a priest, it will be your gift to stand right here close by the bread of life—touching it with your mortal hands, watching up close as hungry people, like yourself, come forward and eat Jesus. It will be your task and gift to see and name the places where God is knitting God's people together, even when the body that is a congregation seems all unraveled and frayed. You will have the gloriously fun work of holy sleuthing, finding the places of God's holy suturing. Maybe think here also with the prophet Ezekiel, from whom St. Paul was borrowing. When the body of God's people seems hopelessly desiccated, you will dwell on and speak to a vision of bones snapping back together and of blood flowing from this hand over here to this other foot over here, even when this hand and this foot hardly seem part of the same body. This bread you will serve enters us, and in difficult as well as in blessedly complicated ways, we are not alone.

In closing, I have to come back to our first reading, from Isaiah. I love the magical and yet worldly specificity of the passage you chose. Isaiah gives us the precise year in chronological time, the number of wings on the seraphs, and even where exactly they placed their wings. Isaiah's response to this vision of the Lord sitting on his throne is first to shout "Woe is me!" I think this is a very helpfully to-the-point passage for those of us called to be priests—for those of us called to have our mouths transformed through holy cauterization.

Isaiah responds:

> "Woe is me! I am lost." Check.
> "For I am a man of unclean lips." Check.
> "And I live among a people of unclean lips!" Definitely check and check.

Yet. Yet. I have seen the Lord here in this temple, right here, with my faltering eyes, Isaiah tells us. And then, a flying seraph brings a live coal and tells Isaiah "Your guilt has departed and your sin is blotted out."

Your guilt has departed. Your sin is blotted out. My guilt has departed. My sin is blotted out.

Kara Nicole Slade, for all the weirdness of this call passage, the wings and the smoke and the shaking thresholds, this word about sin and guilt is the weirdest word. But it is a word that must sustain the possibility of all I have said up to this point. Your guilt has departed. Your sin is blotted out. The very bread that is life, the gift of Christ that is the pulsing heartbeat of each little church and the church universal, that bread, that gift, that immeasurably forgiving blood is also *yours and mine.* And in our ministry, this word of holy freedom may be the hardest word to believe.

Christ be with you, Christ within you, Christ behind you, Christ before you, Christ beside you, Christ to win you, Christ to comfort and restore you.

CHRISTMAS EVE, 2014

Sermon at Trinity United Methodist Church, Durham, North Carolina

Texts: Isaiah 9:2–7; Luke 2:1–20; John 1:1–14

For a child has been born for us, a son given to us. . . . His authority shall grow continually, and there shall be endless peace. . . .

In the beginning was the Word, and the Word was with God, and the Word was God . . . the Light shines in the darkness, and the darkness did not overcome it. . . . And the Word became flesh and lived among us. . . .

In those days a decree went out from Emperor Augustus that all the world should be registered. . . .

Do not be afraid; for see—I am bringing you good news of great joy for all the people. . . .

I want to point out first of all a puzzle that makes Emperor Augustus look silly. Here he is, able to command everyone in the Roman Empire to go to their particular towns of origin in order to be properly counted. And, over here in a little corner of his mighty fancy, hard and bloody-won empire, a child has been born for us, a son given to us.

Later in the service, after singing, we will be coming to the table to receive Jesus, here with us, in the bread and the grape juice. And all over the world, across every empire, Christians will have been or will be soon doing the same thing. So, here is a joke on the mighty emperor. The child who has been born for us, the son given to us, is also here with us, and on church tables across the world. And there is no way any emperor of any empire can keep track of all that. All the world should be registered! Yes. Emperor, sir. And, in this little, hidden place over here where cows are mooing, the whole world has been saved. And that Word that became flesh is going to be right here, in this place, and in uncountable places all over the world.

The Light that shines in the darkness, has come to us in a way that no emperor can order. The emperor cannot demand that the light be counted, or registered, or put under surveillance.

To try to control and count this good news of great joy for all the people—this Word of promise of endless peace—would be like trying to hold the light of the sun in your cupped hands and measure it out evenly.

Silly Emperor Augustus.

My father always worked on Christmas Eve, being a pastor, and we would drive on Christmas Eve night, in the dark, from one small town in Texas to another, to see relatives. I was always too excited to sleep, and my favorite part was watching out the car window to spot way off in the rural distance a farmhouse with their Christmas lights glowing. The parts of Texas we would drive through have flat terrain, so I could see the little lights from far away. They were every bit as magical to me as the Aurora Borealis, even though they had been bought at the local five and dime shop.

I was telling a friend who is Jewish how much I am a sucker still for Christmas lights. I like them in any color and any shape, anywhere. She told me something helpful that has stuck with me. I asked her how she felt about all the lights everywhere this season. She told me that when her kids were little, they had these nifty little glasses that would make every light into a Star of David. They would pile into the car and go look at Christmas lights, through these glasses.

I have friends and family members who wear little pins that say "Put Christ back into Christmas." I think that my friend's Star of David glasses idea is helpful if you want to put the Christ back into Christmas for the next twelve days of Christmas. I am not suggesting you go buy glasses actually to put on to look at lights. I do not mean you necessarily have to go find these specific glasses. But I am suggesting we think about what it means to see Christmas lights, each one, as a sign—maybe as a little focal point, to receive the Light of the whole world.

The Star of David is an apt place to start. Jesus came to bring endless peace to Israel, and through that peace to bless all the nations on the earth. The light begins in Bethlehem and spirals outward, touching every corner of the planet.

Truth is, for some of us, believing that this light touches our own little corner of the planet is even harder than believing that the Middle East will be marked by endless peace. Truth is, envisioning endless peace for Israel, so far away, is easier for some of us than believing our own little lives, in our little corner of the earth, are marked for peace, and lit up by the Word made flesh and the Light made incalculable.

One friend put this to me bluntly after coming back to Durham, having spent the holidays with her siblings somewhere else. Why is it so hard to practice Christian discipleship with one's own family?

My mother is a public school teacher, and one of her favorite lines that a student wrote about some Charles Dickens novel or another was "Families are made of people." This has become a recitation of forbearance in our own family. You know. Families are made of people.

And the Light of the world—the Prince of Peace—has come to save all of the nations through the people of Israel and all of the members of our own fraught and uniquely delightful families.

A group of Christians near to my heart, named the Quakers, affirm that each one of us has within us a light—lit up through the Light that shines in the darkness and is the Word through whom we were, each one us, made.

To see one another this way, as lights of truth and hope, may require a shift in perspective.

A few Sundays ago, when we were singing one of my favorite carols, one little girl in front of me turned her head around, looking up, and then decided to turn her whole body around, and take in the entire ceiling of the church. She seemed to think there was something to be gained by shifting her whole body around to look at parts of the building she had perhaps never taken in before. Seeing one another as lights of the Light of the world may require us to feel and seem about as noticeably childlike, shifting our whole bodies around to see differently.

I want to close with the Gospel according to the *Peanuts Christmas Special*. It may have been a while since you watched it. I highly recommend finding a copy.

Dear Lucy is her usual, bossy self, and she is determined to have the *"Best Christmas Ever!"*

All the gang is there at the party. Charlie Brown is to go find the tree. This is the part that most people remember. A little, scrawny branch is turned into a sparkly little bush. But notice a few things the next time you watch it. The tree does not grow majestically magical, like on a fancy set of the New York Ballet's production of *The Nutcracker Suite*. The scrawny branch is turned into a sparkly little bush.

Then Linus reads the Gospel of Luke. Linus reads the same words we just read here tonight. And then what happens? Families are still made up of people. Lucy does not transform into the Good Fairy in *The Wizard of Oz*. She is still Lucy. And Pigpen is still Pigpen. Snoopy still drools.

But they are together, and something subtly magical has shifted.

And I will tell all of the children here tonight another little Christmas puzzle that is a bit of a joke on some parents and grandparents. This table in front of me, this Lord's Supper where the Word comes to meet us, and be our Light, our light that lights us up in anticipation of everlasting peace . . . .

It does not matter if you have been naughty or nice. There is no "you'd better watch out" when it comes to this gift tonight, for you and for me. You can fuss. You can even cry. It is OK. This gift for us and among us is here.

THE SUNDAY AFTER CHRISTMAS

December 27, 2015

First United Methodist Church, Elgin, Texas
Text: Titus 2:11–14

When my father asked if I would bring you the Word on the Sunday after Christmas, I readily agreed. I mean, he is my dad, and I cannot easily tell him no. And I have heard so many wonderful things about you all from him and from my mom during their time with you. He was bored to tears during retirement, so your need of him was a gift to him. (And to my mom!)

And then, a little later, I asked him about the text. Methodists have assigned texts, as many of you know, and I needed to think and pray ahead of time about the text for this sermon. When he told me the assigned text is from Titus, I wondered what I had gotten myself into.

Titus? I am guessing when you are thinking about Christmas texts, or even any favorite Bible verse, Titus does not readily come to mind.

There are lots of children here today. I have a puzzle for you. In order to keep yourself from being bored during the sermon, try to find the book of Titus in your pew Bible. Try finding the book of Titus without going to the table of contents.

The New Testament letter we call Titus is like a little box from a great aunt who always sends her gifts early. She sends her gifts so early that her little gifts are first under the tree and so also the last to be found. This tiny little gift that was left under the tree, this gift called Titus, is a gift that could have been left there, unopened.

We are lucky that the dog did not find it and rip it to shreds before we took the tree down.

But, while taking the tree down, we do find this little box of Titus. So we open it now on the third day of Christmas. And now, reading through this little New Testament letter, we sort of wish that the dog had actually found it and torn it to shreds.

The passage assigned is uncontroversial enough. It is about grace, appearing to all, making us "self-controlled, upright, and godly," a people "zealous for good deeds."

If you just stick to the assigned verses, you might stitch them onto a tea towel or put them on a coffee mug. But you would have to make sure not to read any of the verses around this one little bit of this little scrap of a gift that is Titus.

If you read what comes right before this little section of this little letter, it is a showstopper.

Slaves be obedient to your masters. Do not even appear to roll your eyes when your master tells you what to do. Wives be obedient to your husbands. If you are not obedient, you will give God a bad name. Anyone who is in leadership—bishops, elders, etc., must be totally above reproach.

Do not shame anyone. Impress everyone with your purity and obedience toward anyone above you.

So, here we go. I am going to try this morning to wrestle some Good News out of this little scrap of a letter we have in the New Testament. The dog did not tear it to shreds. It remained under the tree, uneaten, so we now have to deal with it.

In the 1950s there was a Methodist magazine called *Together*. This magazine was quite glossy and impressive. It was an example of Methodists trying to compete with the likes of *Time* or *Life* magazines. *Together* ran a series of competitions each year for about a decade called "The Methodist Family of the Year!" You were supposed to look across the aisle, at a pew near you, and discern whether you would want someone representing your church in the district competition. A congregation would nominate a family to compete, then the competition would move outward from congregation to district to conference—ultimately to the national competition. Can you imagine? You were to look around, appraising one another, determining whose family was pure enough, upright enough, to be the Methodist Family of the Year!

I think we can all agree this was a bad idea. I sure do not want my family being appraised in that way, and it probably was not good for overall amity in a congregation for people to be checking one another off a list of ambassadorial fitness.

Maybe Titus made its way into the Bible because being Christian and being an ambassador for Jesus in this world is just so confusing. How do we live "zealous for good deeds," without betraying the very gospel that is the source of our abiding grace?

We just celebrated Christmas. Let's start there.

On our drive from North Carolina to Texas we went over what felt like the longest bridge on earth. It goes along the southern edge of Louisiana, on Highway Ten. Once we finally got over the longest bridge on earth, we needed to find a place to use the bathroom. There was one available, and it was a truck stop. I am going to admit to you all right now that I stopped there only because it was the only available spot. I was being quite the snob as we pulled into the parking lot. The station had a casino adjacent, even. Really? A casino? Lord.

As I was leaving this place, this place that was offering me much needed hospitality, I had one of those visions that God sometimes gives me. God is sometimes not subtle with me, like I need a neon sign rather than a whisper.

I realized, Jesus was born at a Pilot gas station, with a casino adjacent, and with the shower numbers being called out over a loud speaker so that Santa can take a shower.

Luke's story of the birth of Jesus is pretty clear about this. There was no place respectable to have a baby, so Mary gave birth to the Light of the World in a barn, with cow poo. The Gospel of Matthew has a version of this weirdness too. The book begins explaining Jesus' lineage. Jesus' family tree has not only mothers with questionable pregnancies but also what we might call women of ill repute.

This story we just celebrated two days ago is not a story of respectability.

During the time that Titus was written, the Roman Empire was flailing around to secure its waning prominence. If you have seen films of Germany during the Third Reich or Italy during fascism or Maoist China, with lines of men marching in unison to show strength, you can have some idea about how the Roman Empire functioned. The term "boots on the ground" has serious meaning for how the Roman Empire maintained order. They had many boots on the ground. Boys were trained for war from the beginning of their little boy lives. Girls were born to be women who would give birth to boys to be trained for war.

Then Jesus comes into all of this, and takes hold. The gospel was originally spread by and among women. And that was a problem. If women started teaching their little boys something different about their lives, this could disrupt the whole system.

How do Christians now try to be ambassadors for a man in the Roman Empire who was killed for being an offense to the empire?

Well, we declare him as our savior. "For the grace of God has appeared, bringing salvation to all."

The next question Christians seem perennially tempted to ask is this one: "But, do we *look* saved?"

And one answer to this question is *Yes!* We looked saved! Look at us! Do we not have good teenagers who attend Sunday school every week? Do we not have the right Sunday school clothing? Do we not have good Sunday school marriages and yards and jobs? Do we not wear good, Christian, James Avery jewelry?

We are so close to Austin here in Elgin. So I need to name another, related temptation. Another answer to "Do we look saved?" is slightly different, and it can turn into its own sort of weird. YES! We are saved! We do not shop at malls! We buy only organic! We hate Walmart! We do not have televisions! We look saved!

This little gift that the dog did not eat names so very clearly the danger of losing the gospel. And here is the thing that troubles me most. If we become intent to be ambassadors for Jesus by trying to look saved, we will make ourselves into a people who turn away the very same people who need the gospel the most. We will subtly discourage sinners—sinners like us—from coming to church.

Jesus was born in a Pilot gas station stall. We are saved by a baby, born in a manger. Born as part of a family with a checkered past.

Praise be to God.